Follow the Blue Lin
John W. Hayes

R & D Business Publi......g
Unit 3, Cleethorpes Business Centre,
Jackson Place,
Grimsby,
North East Lincolnshire.
DN36 4AS.

First published in Great Britain in 2018

Copyright © John W. Hayes

The right of John W. Hayes to be identified as the Author has been asserted in accordance with the Copyright, Design, and Patents Act 1988.

All rights reserved. No part of this publication may be reproduced, stored in a retrieval system, or transmitted in any form or by any means, whether electronic, mechanical, photocopying, recording, or otherwise without the prior written permission of the Publisher. This book may not be lent, resold, hired out, or otherwise disposed of by way of trade in any form of binding or cover other than that in which it is published without the prior written consent of the Publisher.

No responsibility for loss occasioned to any person or corporate body acting or refraining to act as a result of reading material in this book can be accepted by the Publisher, by the Author, or by the employer(s) of the Author.

ISBN: 9781719820257

Table of Contents

About the Author 1
A Doer, Not a Planner 2
Disclaimer 5
The Ecovia do Litoral 7
The Blue Line 12
The Portugal Pie Eaters 14
The Best Laid Plans of Mice and Middle-Aged Men in Lycra 19
Denied Boarding 23
I Hear the Train Coming 25
Vila Real de Santo António 28
The Grand Départ 30
The Financial Crisis 33
The Kindness of Strangers #1 37
An Explosive Start 39
The Big Storm 45
Cabanas De Tavira 51
The Power of Community 61
Snakes on a Bike 64
Fighting Crime 66

Fuseta – Not Such a "Relaxing" Place 69
Lost in Time.. 71
A Broken Promise... 74
Ola Olhão... 77
Le Bonk 79
The Best 99p A Cyclist Can Spend 82
Escaping Faro 86
The Second Financial Crisis................................. 93
The Blind Leading the Blind.............................. 100
Quick Sand... 104
Death by Golf.. 106
Breakfast in Vilamoura 110
Stopping for Beers in Albufeira......................... 112
Rude Lady 122
Fear of the Dark 125
Deep Heat.. 133
Praia da Luz... 136
The Kindness of Strangers #2............................ 138
The Kindness of Strangers #3............................ 140
How Much Can You Bench Press?................... 143
Super Supermarkets 144

Where Did Those Hills Come From? 147

The Germans, the Australians, and the Albufeira Cycling Club.. 149

Praia da Salema... 152

Surf's Up 155

Into The Wind.. 157

The Long Ride Back 162

Coming Down.. 165

An Education.. 170

Online Fundraising: Five Tips for Success 173

Acknowledgments.. 177

About MegaSport Travel..................................... 179

About the Author

John W. Hayes started cycling as an antidote to his largely sedentary professional life in online marketing. Short rides along the seafront of his hometown of Cleethorpes in North East Lincolnshire, where he lives with his partner, Sarah, and their two daughters, Rose and Dotty, soon progressed to longer journeys out into the countryside.

Although he would never break any records for speed, his desire to travel further by bike became ever more persuasive until he eventually completed a 100-mile (160-kilometre) ride in a single day. Describing himself as more of a lifestyle and leisure cyclist than a MAMIL (Middle-Aged Man in Lycra), the 100-mile ride included a visit to a fish and chip shop, a pub, and a long lie-down in a field.

With 100 miles in the bag, he was drawn to longer and more adventurous rides wherever possible, chasing the sun. He now tries to ride every day (regardless of the weather) and clocks-up a minimum of 100 miles in the saddle each week as part of the #100MileBikeCommute social media initiative he created as part of an evangelical urge to get more people cycling.

A Doer, Not a Planner

I've always considered myself more of a doer than a planner. At work, I tend to run at things, relying on experience, gut instinct, and nervous energy to get me through 80 percent of the day. The rest of the time is set aside for chaos – this makes things fun and keeps me on my toes. I work on the principle that, while planners just talk about stuff, doers get things done. Sometimes, this rather gung-ho approach to life gets me into trouble. But, what the heck! Rules, like my unfortunate wheel rims (well, this *is* a book about cycling) were made for bending.

It was perhaps down to this spirit of simply doing things that I found myself alone at Faro Airport. It wasn't part of the plan – if there ever was such a thing – to arrive in Portugal alone. There should have been two of us.

I'd arranged via a series of messages on Facebook (I'm really not a phone person) to meet my younger brother, Allan, at the airport. I hadn't seen him for a couple of years and was looking forward to catching up with him and learning all about his new life in Northern Ireland, where he'd recently been relocated for work. I hoped we'd reconnect while enjoying some leisurely, long-distance cycling in the sunshine, interspersed with the odd beer and the occasional glass of red wine. I couldn't think of a better way to spend a long weekend.

Allan was due to fly out of Belfast, arriving 30 minutes after my flight from East Midland's airport touched down. I should have been waiting for him – undoubtedly enjoying the buzz from the first of many *bica* (Portugal's slightly longer answer to an espresso). Unfortunately, upon inspection of Allan's somewhat crumpled but very clean passport (it had been through the washing machine), the lovely people at EasyJet's check-in desk had a very different idea, and he was denied boarding.

Allan – the planner, the map reader, the linguist, the man who could have saved me from financial ruin, dehydration, and appalling sunburn – would not be joining me. This book is dedicated to Allan. All the misadventures, the moments of sheer despair, and the occasional tear (and yes, there were a few of them) are the fault of my darling younger brother.

Actually, I shouldn't be too harsh on Allan. When push comes to shove, he's as useless as I am (as clearly demonstrated by his freshly-laundered passport). If he would have made it down to the Algarve, we'd have probably both died.

My first trip across the Algarve almost ended at Faro Airport. Dressed awkwardly in Lycra, clutching an overstuffed set of panniers, a cycle helmet balanced on my head, the remnants of my previous year's holiday money (25 euros) in my pocket, and thoroughly alone, I seriously contemplated getting on the first plane back to the UK.

But, remember – I'm a doer, not a planner, and this was going to be a great adventure. I think I probably told myself this more than 100 times as I jumped on my bike for the short ride into Faro and my connecting train journey to the starting point at Vila Real de Santo António.

Disclaimer

This book could have just as easily been titled, How Not to Cycle the Algarve. It's actually based on numerous attempts at the route but focuses mainly on my first – albeit unplanned – disastrous solo expedition in 2012 and two more successful but nonetheless traumatic (fun) trips made with equally unprepared friends in 2014 and 2018. Other stories are taken from shorter rides along the various stretches of the route while holidaying in the region with my family.

If you're looking for a cycling book documenting the efforts of finely-tuned athletes, pushing themselves beyond acceptable barriers of pain to cross vast distances at a ridiculous pace, this probably isn't the book for you. For a more gnarly read, perhaps I can recommend you pick up the excellent Life Cycles by Julian Sayarer or the equally enjoyable The Man Who Cycled the World by Mark Beaumont. Both of these gentlemen's epic global journeys make my jaunts across Portugal look like a holiday (which, of course, they were).

This book is for the rest of us, whose dreams and abilities are perhaps a little less extreme. If you like the idea of getting lost on a bike for a couple of days in the glorious sunshine, lubricating your inner mechanisms with the occasional cheeky beer along the route, and just not taking yourself too seriously (how could anyone take themselves too seriously in cycle shorts?), then stick around – I promise you, it'll be emotional.

The Ecovia do Litoral

There's no need for the hard sell here. Why would anyone not want to go cycling in the Algarve? But if you want me to put my Algarve Tourist Board hat on, here goes:

The Ecovia do Litoral (the coastal eco-way) is a cycle route which, as the name suggests, follows the coast across the beautiful Algarve region of southern Portugal. The route stretches some 214 kilometres (133 miles) from the frontier town of Vila Real de Santo António on the Spanish border to the dramatic, 75-metre-high cliff tops of Cape St. Vincent on Europe's most southwestern tip. The multi-surface route, encompassing (mainly quiet) roads, dedicated cycle paths, and dirt tracks (of various quality), takes in pretty much everything the Algarve has to offer, from sleepy fishing villages to bustling tourist resorts, cosmopolitan cities (Faro), and some of the best (and most expensive) golf real estate in Europe.

The Ecovia also takes in many hidden treasures, mostly unseen by the millions of tourists who visit the region each year and stick like glue to the beach or the golf course. These include thousands of acres of orange, lemon, and olive groves, the curious frozen moonscapes formed by the region's famous coastal salt pans, and the seemingly bone-dry, yet highly fertile, small agricultural holdings where modern-day farming practices have yet to make an impact.

The route is incredibly accessible. The majority of the ride is on the flat, with only the occasional and mostly non-challenging hills (meaning, there are a couple of killers along the way), enabling riders of all abilities to tackle the journey. Seriously, my 70-year-old parents-in-law have completed the ride over five days, so what's your excuse?

The abundance of budget flights into Faro from across the UK and Europe and cheap accommodation (particularly, out-of-season) also makes the long weekend trip (required to complete the journey at a comfortable pace) very affordable.

Regarding expenses, I've personally done the ride for less than £500, including flights, bike hire, hotels, and spending money. However, it could be done for much less if you swapped the hotels for campsites and fuelled your ride at supermarkets along the way instead of stopping at bars, cafes, and restaurants.

Naturally, it's also possible to spend a bit more (or in some cases, a *lot* more) money on the ride. There are a number of companies who will help you do this by providing all manner of package deals, including airport transfers, luggage forwarding services, and even tour guides. It's just a case of what you are comfortable paying for and your level of confidence on the road.

For cyclists looking for a halfway house between complete independence and a little security, it's always worth checking whether your bike hire company offers roadside assistance, should you have any mechanical problems or emotional meltdowns.

I personally like the feeling of "roughing it" and the greater sense of achievement you get when you do things independently – but I won't judge you if you want to make the ride a little more comfortable. There is already too much snobbery in cycling – let's leave that nonsense for those cyclists who haven't yet found their way off the golf course.

The route is served by an excellent – if not rather slow – train service which runs from Vila Real de Santo António on the Spanish border to the town of Lagos in the west, some 34 kilometres short of the route's end. Bike carriage is free, and tickets are cheap (certainly as compared to the UK), providing excellent insurance against any mechanical issues, injuries, or plain old bouts of laziness.

Note: *If you don't want to tackle the whole ride, cycling between stations and then letting the train take the strain for a while is also a great option.*

The weather, the scenery, the food, the wine, and the people you meet along the Ecovia (all detailed in this book) make the Algarve a very special place. In fact, I couldn't think of anywhere else in the world where I would rather ride my bike.

That is not to say everything is perfect with the Ecovia and this is where a little better planning would come in handy.

The Ecovia is not well-mapped (at least, not on paper). This was a fact first highlighted to me by a visit to a Tourist Information Centre on a family holiday prior to tackling the ride for the first time. I was reliably informed that because the route had only recently opened (some three years prior), nobody had quite gotten around to producing a map yet. More than a decade later, I've still not seen a paper map of the route.

Note: *On our last ride, I employed the detailed routes found on the excellent Bikemap.net website, which can be downloaded and followed easily on the equally excellent BikeGPX smartphone app (available for free from the Google Play Store and Apple App Store).*

The lack of maps wouldn't be a problem if the route was clearly marked. In places, the signage is excellent. However, this experience is not guaranteed. For example, the blue line referenced in the title of this book (a navigational aid marking the road sections of the route) can lead you into a false sense of security.

The Blue Line

I was first made aware of the blue line when I initially discussed the idea of cycling the Ecovia with my father-in-law. As a regular visitor to the Algarve, he told me the route was nice and easy and clearly marked (he'd recently completed a 30km stretch himself).

He reliably informed me, "Just follow the blue line, and you won't go wrong."

Sadly, the blue line isn't always so reliable. One minute, it's there, and the next, it's gone. If a road has ever been resurfaced, you can bet your bottom dollar that the blue line will be hidden under the fresh layer of asphalt and has never been repainted. Typically, the blue line always seems to disappear at road junctions, and the most obvious onward route is nearly always wrong. As your eyes adjust to the bright Portuguese sunshine, you can sometimes make out the outline of where the blue line used to be. Reconnecting with the blue line after a period in the wilderness can become something of a celebration – albeit a short-lived one.

The blue line is supplemented by an assortment of other navigational aids ranging from detailed metal signs, bike symbols, and the occasional roughly spray-painted arrow (normally yellow) on trees, walls, and rocks. Apparently, the various municipal authorities responsible for maintaining the route couldn't come up with a more uniform system. Perhaps more frustratingly, the route occasionally – and without warning – just ends, with new construction sites and high wire fences forcing the rider to find alternative paths.

In my mind, this just adds to the charm of the route. In our ordinary lives, most of us follow the same old, boring paths every day. I personally like the idea of feeling a little lost every now and again. My lack of planning skills certainly helped out in this direction.

In many ways, I share a number of personality traits with the Ecovia. We are both fairly easy-going, a little shambolic at times, and very much a work in progress. Shouldn't life *always* be very much a work in progress?

The Portugal Pie Eaters

Before we cycle too far along this route, I wanted to take the opportunity to introduce the various other characters who played such an important role in this book.

While I am very comfortable riding by myself (as I did – albeit unplanned – in 2012), riding in the company of good friends almost certainly helps create more memories and definitely made documenting and writing this book a lot easier and a lot more fun. I think that when you cycle by yourself, it's just a case of getting the job done. Not that this isn't enjoyable but more often than not, the act of cycling isn't really the full story.

It's also worth saying that while my younger brother, Allan, never made the ride, the guys who did are now as close to me as brothers.

The Portugal Pie Eaters were named after the WhatsApp Group used to plan (again, using the word "plan" in the loosest of terms) the 2018 ride on – and, in many ways, the name perfectly describes our athletic form.

The Portugal Pie Eaters are:

- **Big Iain:** One of my oldest friends; I've known this guy since college. We shared a flat in Aberdeen and started our professional lives together on the same day at the same newspaper (we sold advertising) before heading off along different career paths. Iain joined me on the ride in 2014 and 2018. While Iain thoroughly enjoyed the ride in 2014, he did struggle on some sections and turned down the opportunity of a similar long-distance ride the following year. I wasn't sure if Iain would ever join me out on the road again but shortly after myself and Dave announced our 2018 ride via social media, he called me out of the blue. Iain was very drunk. He told me that he loved me, and that he wanted to join the ride. I couldn't have been happier. The absolutely brilliant thing is, Iain actually crushed the hills on his second attempt and regularly led our little peloton.

- **Big Euan:** A big character with an infectious sense of enthusiasm. Euan came along on the 2014 ride and acted as our chief navigator. Despite the fact that I had cycled much of the route several times before, I somehow believed Euan – who had never previously set foot in Portugal –

might know the route a little better than me. I put this down to the fact that Iain – who had worked alongside Euan for a number of years – told me that Euan was a great outdoorsman. This, I believed, meant he could read a map. When you are cycling along a coastal route where the sea is always to your left, you wouldn't believe how spectacularly lost we became under Euan's leadership. What Euan lacked in navigational skills, he certainly made up for in diplomacy. Euan never complained, always wore a smile on his face, and, although only in Portugal for a few days, he insisted on trying to learn a few words of Portuguese, sampling the local cuisine, and taking a real interest in the country and its people.

- **Big Dave:** Our token millennial, and the catalyst for the 2018 ride. At the time he committed to the ride, Dave didn't even own a bike and hadn't ridden one since childhood. One of the first lessons Dave learned about cycling was to not always believe everything I say. This was particularly true in the case of a statement I made about there being no hills in Portugal. In my defence, I must have forgotten about them (don't they say something similar about the pain of childbirth?). He latterly started comparing me to the infamous war criminal, Chemical Ali – a "stooge" of the Iraqi dictator Saddam Hussein, and a man who fervently denied that American tanks had breached Iraqi defences during the Gulf War and the subsequent fall of Baghdad. The second lesson Dave learned about cycling was that hours spent training in the gym on a stationary bike don't compare to any time on the road on a real bike. All through the ride, Dave told me he would never get back on a bike again. Despite this, Dave regularly joins in on chats on the WhatsApp group to discuss next year's ride. I give him six months before he buys himself a bike and starts putting in some real training miles.

- **Ginger Chris:** Another friend from my youth, Chris is one of the funniest and most considerate people I know. He is the kind of guy you would trust with your life. However, he also has a bit of a lunatic streak about him (all in the name of fun), which could quite easily shave a few years off your life as well (although I'm sure it would be totally worth it). Chris joined the ride in 2018 and, despite not having ridden in several years and falling off his bike in a quite spectacular fashion within the first kilometre of the ride, almost instantly found himself in a happy place. I personally lost count of how many times Chris told me how much he was enjoying the ride. Out of everyone I have ridden with, Chris is the one guy I would go to first if we were to take on a more challenging ride – maybe involving camping. When consulting Chris about this book, he told me that, rather than focusing on his girth (which is as considerable as any other member of the group), he would prefer it if I singled him out for being ginger.

- **Wee Allan:** My younger brother, who is conspicuous in this book only because of his absence. One day, Allan, I will make you do this ride, and whether you like it or not, you will enjoy it.

The Best Laid Plans of Mice and Middle-Aged Men in Lycra

Okay, as I've already alluded, planning is not my forte, but it would be impossible and somewhat foolish to undertake such a journey without a little research. What can I say? I'm a fool.

Cycling the Algarve had been a pipedream of mine for some time. Some might describe the ride as an item on my bucket list that I was desperate to tick off, but I refuse to use that phrase – until, at the very least, I receive a terminal diagnosis. For months prior to my first trip, I had poured over the same old, often amateur-produced websites detailing the route. Like a kid staring at his dream bike in his mother's mail order catalogue, I consumed everything I could about the route without digesting any real information. As poor as much of the information was, I should have at least taken a few notes as I browsed.

I didn't.

My planning was limited to a cheap – and quite frankly, useless – road map purchased on Amazon, which didn't even feature many of the minor roads on the Algarve, let alone the actual cycle route itself, and an out-of-date train timetable printed from the Internet. Using the map and my thumb as a unit of measurement, I divided the route into three similar-sized chunks and jumped online to book hotels in Vila Real de Santo António, Faro, Praia da Rocha, and one last night again in Faro.

For some time, I'd actually been considering camping along the route. I think this had more to do with my desire to prove myself as a real man (surely, an early symptom of an imminent mid-life crisis) rather than to get closer to nature. I had spent weeks agonizing whether or not to buy a Topeak Bikamper tent (Google it; it's fantastic), but the bargain-bucket prices of out-of-season hotel accommodation on the Algarve made camping look like an expensive option. Four nights' accommodation barely broke £100. I would later learn that pre-paying for all my accommodation would be the smartest thing I did in the run-up to my little adventure.

As I get older, the thought of camping along the route becomes ever more persuasive. I hope to God that I never submit to these desires.

My lack of planning certainly did not limit the amount of kit I tried to squeeze into my Raleigh panniers – procured, again, for a bargain price on Amazon (is there anything they don't sell?). I'm actually a little embarrassed by the amount of gear I hauled around Portugal that never saw the light of day on my first trip. This included a camera, an iPad, a Kindle eReader, and, of course, my smartphone – which could have easily performed all the tasks I needed the other devices for, as well as replacing my next-to-useless map. I even packed a spare pair of shoes and – at the insistence of my partner, who was keen to remind me "it gets chilly at night" – a thick woolly jumper, just in case.

What was I thinking?

I've since honed my packing strategy to the bare minimum, knowing that I can always pick things up along the route as needed.

Even with my overstuffed panniers, the plan (there's that word again!) was to buy essential items like sunblock, toothpaste, and other toiletries in Portugal, so my panniers could come aboard the aircraft as hand luggage and help keep the price of my budget flights to a minimum. I had a handful of Euros saved over from a previous year's holiday which would get me from the airport to my first night's accommodation, and therefore, I didn't have an immediate need for any local currency. As a popular tourist destination, there wouldn't be any problem finding a bank machine along the route once these initial funds had run out.

Our bikes for the journey were hired online via a company called MegaSport (https://megasportravel.com).

The robust, hybrid bikes were to be delivered to meet our flights at Faro airport. The process of booking was relatively painless, and all the details were confirmed by email. MegaSport would also provide us with a set of basic tools, a puncture repair kit, a spare inner tube, bike locks, a pump, and a phone number, in case anything should go wrong.

What could possibly go wrong?

Denied Boarding

I learned of Allan's passport dilemma while boarding my flight. Halfway up the aircraft steps, I received a somewhat confused phone call, explaining his predicament. As I took my seat, I suggested he should go straight back into Belfast and head to the passport office, where he'd be able to get a replacement document and fly out the next day. As the aircraft doors closed, and my mobile switched to flight mode, I convinced myself it wouldn't be so bad. I'd do the first leg of the trip by myself. Half the route I already knew well from holidaying in the area. Then, I would meet Allan in Faro. The holiday was still most definitely on.

I'll admit the prospect of doing even part of the trip by myself excited me. Then, it terrified me. Upon landing in Faro, I turned my phone back on, optimistically hoping for good news. It never came.

To the best of my knowledge, Allan still hasn't gotten a new passport.

I don't know why, but I hung around the airport until all the passengers from the Belfast flight had disembarked and cleared passport control. The thought that Allan could have been winding me up and was about to make a surprise appearance somewhat optimistically crossed my mind. He wasn't, and he didn't. I picked up my panniers, strapped them to my bike, and pushed off.

As I tried to find my bearings to exit the confines of Faro Airport's car park and head into the city, I passed a group of statues, positioned rather comically on a roundabout and staring into the sky at the incoming and departing aircraft. Perhaps they were also waiting for Allan.

Note: *if you are planning on taking your own bike to Portugal, Faro Airport has a number of bike assembly points positioned by the luggage carousels and check-in desks, complete with work stands, tools, and pumps. This is something I've never seen in any other airport and perhaps best demonstrates Portugal's commitment to growing cycle tourism. Nice work, Faro Airport.*

I Hear the Train Coming

The train service that serves the Algarve is pretty basic. Don't expect a first-class carriage, catering, or even a trolley service. The rolling stock is similar to the suburban or metropolitan services offered in many large cities and is often covered in graffiti. But what the trains lack in comfort and speed, they certainly make up for in value. Bikes are carried free of charge in the rear compartment of the train, which comes equipped with space-saving hooks to hang four cycles by their front wheels. The doors for the rear compartments manually slide open, and, depending which stations you board or alight from, can be some distance from the exceptionally low platforms. This can make loading your fully-loaded bike difficult – although train guards or fellow cyclists are usually only too happy to help.

The service, which runs along a single track, was originally built to serve the needs of the agricultural community before mass tourism took over the Algarve. This means the stations can be some distance from the coast – not a problem, if you have a bike. It also means the service misses out some larger tourist destinations on the Algarve, including Vilamoura.

However, the single line can lead to significant delays as trains wait in stations to let others pass. In my experience, the trains never run on time – but, seriously, what's your hurry? As you wait for your train (which you will hear long before you see), you're as likely to see someone walking a horse down the line as anything that resembles a high-speed rail service. Nothing moves particularly fast in the Algarve (a bit like my cycling speed), especially in the east – which is maybe why I like it so much.

Taking the train is an excellent introduction to rural life in the Algarve. It also serves as a reminder that, away from the luxury villas, marinas, and golf courses, Portugal is not a wealthy country – at least, not in fiscal terms. However, if you judge the success of a nation by the friendliness of its population, the weather, the food, and the culture, it might just be one of the wealthiest places I have ever been.

I've had the pleasure of speaking to numerous local cyclists as we've helped each other on and off the trains all along the Algarve. Most of the people I have met do not fall into the demographic category of the middle-class MAMILs – who appear to make up the bulk of the cyclists I encounter at home, pushing their way towards a personal best (or PB) – on their commute to and from the office.

The bikes hauled up onto the trains are often rusty with worn saddles covered with the obligatory plastic bag. One gentleman I chatted with had a bike with a missing pedal; a rudimentary metal spike replaced the missing component. I'm guessing a lot of these people are – and I hate to use the term – quite poor.

However, virtually all these fellow cyclists have spoken almost perfect English and enthusiastically asked questions about my rides in the country. They have offered advice, passed on their best wishes, and have nearly always worn a smile on their faces while helping me take my bike down from the train.

The more cynical amongst you might think this kindness is doled out in the hope of some reward. In my experience, you'd be wrong (shame on you!). Perhaps people are just more helpful in this part of the world. And, let's face facts: Nobody is nicer than your fellow cyclists.

If you can get a window free of graffiti, be sure to keep an eye out for the flamingos and other exotic birdlife that flock to the wetlands around Monte Gordo, one stop before the ride's starting point in Vila Real de Santo António.

Vila Real de Santo António

Vila Real de Santo António is a charming city nestled on the Rio Guadiana, separating Portugal from its neighbour, Spain. The city built its fortune on tuna and sardine fisheries, but now, like most of the Algarve, it relies on tourism to pay the bills. Despite the opening of the Guadiana International Bridge in 1991 which connects the two countries, a ferry still runs from Vila Real to Ayamonte on the Spanish side of the river and attracts considerable traffic from tourists, as well as many Spanish residents who are tempted across the river by the lower prices and hospitality Vila Real has to offer.

The ferry is also a great opportunity for any cyclists who want to start their ride in another country. At just a couple of euros for your crossing, the ferry offers perhaps one of the cheapest multi-country travel experiences available anywhere.

While Ayamonte on the Spanish side has a bit of a reputation as a soulless border town (rather unfairly, in my opinion) – starting your ride with some authentic Spanish tapas at a street café on the Plaza de la Lagunas can be a real treat. It doesn't matter how many of the small dishes you order; the waiters will never write anything down, and, certainly in my experience, never fail to bring the right food to your table. Seriously, you should challenge them. Perhaps there is an opportunity here for the waiters to train the staff at my local branch of Costa Coffee, where I once returned a cup of black coffee four times because they couldn't get their heads around not adding milk.

Note: *If you are planning to take the ferry across to Spain, it is important to remember that the one-hour time difference between Portugal and Spain can confuse your understanding of the ferry's timetable, particularly around siesta time or evening services.*

The Grand Départ

Vila Real's thriving retail and restaurant scene was bolstered upon my arrival by the annual Feira de Praia – an incredibly popular outdoor market and travelling funfair, which dates back to 1765 and takes over much of the city centre, selling a vast range craftwork, handmade clothing, and artisan foodstuffs.

As a general rule of thumb, the higher quality and more authentic items on sale at the Feira de Praia can be found in Vila Real's main central square. Don't let the tackier items on the market's periphery put you off from exploring in more detail.

Arriving late in the day, I checked into the pleasant, three-star Hotel Apolo and locked my bike in the hotel's secure bike storage facility (a shed lined with space-saving bike-storage hooks similar to those found on the train) before heading out for a small beer and a tosta mista (cheese and ham toasty).

In 2018, while hanging the bikes in the shed, Chris somehow managed to knock all four bikes from the hooks and strangle himself between the twisted cycles. Tears of laughter rolled down our faces as we rushed to his assistance, alerted by the crash of steel bikes and his weak cries for help. After falling off at the airport and almost decapitating himself in Vila Real, I wasn't sure if Chris was going to make the first 50 km, let alone the entire route.

Back in 2012, with the Feira de Praia in full swing, Vila Real was packed with locals, tourists, and visitors from across the border. That night wouldn't be a good time to find a table for one, so I consumed my tosta mista in the relative anonymity of the crowds around the market stalls. Promising myself an early start, I ordered a second tosta and perhaps a second or third (okay, fourth) small beer before taking myself back to my hotel for an early night.

The plan for the first day of the ride without Allan hadn't really changed too much. I would start the day with a quick visit to the bank to grab some euros, hit a local supermarket to buy last-minute essentials, and be on the road by around 9.30 AM. If everything ran according to schedule (ha!), I'd arrive at the halfway point in Tavira around lunchtime and grab something to eat, avoiding the worst of the midday heat, before pushing on to Faro, where I'd arrive sometime later in the afternoon, just in time for dinner.

Trust me; the plan (which was primarily governed by my belly) was so simple, it almost wrote itself.

As it turned out, making meal times would be the least of my problems. Actually being able to *buy* food would be problematic enough.

The Financial Crisis

In 2012, Europe was in the grip of a financial crisis. The financial pages of the newspapers at the time weren't offering a very optimistic outlook for much of the continent, often referring to the worst-affected countries as PIGS (Portugal, Ireland, Greece, and Spain). Greece teetered on the brink of total collapse. The Cypriot government had taken money from the country's private bank accounts to bail out the country. In Ireland, newly-built housing estates were left abandoned, and in Spain, unemployment soared. Things weren't looking too rosy in Portugal, either, where I was about to experience my own mini-financial meltdown.

With the sun rapidly climbing in the sky, Factor 50 sunblock was high on my shopping list, alongside bottled water and some bananas (high-energy food). I hit the bank and asked for 200 euros, only to find my card was declined. I walked along the street and hit another bank – same deal. The same thing happened at the next two banks I visited.

Confused, I went back to my hotel to jump online (I knew there was a good reason to pack the iPad) and check my bank account via the free

Wi-Fi in the lobby. I'd just been paid a considerable amount for a freelance gig I was working on (around 3 months' salary), so I definitely wasn't short on money. Then, I noticed that the equivalent of 800 euros had been taken from my account that very morning. In a panic, I called the Clydesdale Bank.

It took me around 30 minutes to get to the bottom of my issue.

Apparently, the lack of available funds was entirely my own fault. I hadn't notified my bank that I was travelling abroad, and so, in the interest of security, they had not authorised my attempts to withdraw cash. This confused me. I travel a lot for both work and pleasure and had never informed the bank about my travels before.

I was reliably informed, "It's a new thing."

In this day and age, you would think the issue could have been settled with a few keystrokes and the click of a mouse. Apparently, because I'd made multiple attempts to withdraw cash, my account had been flagged as at risk, and, because it was a Friday and it would take one working day to fix, nothing could be done about it until Monday.

I took a deep breath and calmly explained my situation. I was alone in Portugal with 50 miles between each of my hotel stays, and just a couple of euro cents to my name. What could the Clydesdale Bank do to help me?

The answer was crushing:

Absolutely nothing!

I asked to speak with a supervisor. There wasn't one available.

The thing that really upset me was the passive-aggressive tone my call handler possessed. She used polite words, but you could tell she was really pissed-off with her life working in a call centre and listening to wankers like me every day. I could imagine her thinking: *This guy is sunning himself in Portugal; what does he have to complain about?* And then, concluding: *I'm going to spoil his day.*

The call was terminated with the chirpy customer service agent saying, "Is there anything else we can help you with today, Sir?"

Perhaps she should have rephrased that closing statement to: "Is there *anything* we can help you with today, Sir?"

It turns out the answer was: "No."

I really hope this book sells well. Not for reasons of fame or fortune, but just to highlight to as many people as possible how badly an organisation like the Clydesdale Bank can treat a loyal client.

Screw you, Clydesdale Bank. When a customer who has banked with you for 35+ years, always maintained their account in good standing, and clearly has the funds available asks you for help, you bloody well help them!

I look forward to receiving a grovelling apology from their PR department following the publication of this book. The question is: How do you compensate someone for mental anguish, sunburn, and anything else I can think of to shame them? Perhaps they can purchase a bulk order of this book and use it as a customer service training aid.

I won't hold my breath.

The Kindness of Strangers #1

While I was rather publicly ranting at the Clydesdale Bank's customer service representative, a fellow guest approached me. He was an English gentleman who looked to be enjoying the early years of his retirement in the sun. He apologised for listening to my conversation and asked if there was any way he could help. We talked through my problem for a few minutes before finding a solution.

It turned out he was a semi-retired antique dealer who now lived in Spain. He was in Portugal to find new stock which he would sell (mainly to UK customers) via eBay. As an occasional eBay trader myself, I knew the gentleman would have a PayPal account for accepting online payments. I quickly logged into my own account and found that I had amassed £68 of credit – which, with his permission, I promptly forwarded to him in exchange for five crisp 20-euro notes (he gave me a good exchange rate).

In all seriousness, I think he would have insisted on giving me the money regardless of my ability to pay him there and then. I don't know if it is the sunshine, the glorious sight of a bicycle (man's finest invention), or the pathetic sight of a slightly overweight man in his forties, clad in Lycra, but there is something about long-distance bike rides that brings out the kindness of strangers. This is something I would discover time and time again along this route (all detailed in this book).

With 100 euros in my wallet and all my hotels pre-paid online, I had the security of knowing that I would be able to, at the very least, feed and hydrate myself over the next three days, but I had little financial back-up in case of emergency. Travelling by myself, this was a concern. I called home and asked my partner, Sarah, to send me another £300 via Western Union (just in case).

An Explosive Start

For weeks, building up to the trip, I'd been wondering how we would mark the start of our ride. Would I share a motivational speech with my younger sibling? Would we toast the journey with a clink of two tiny cups of bica? Would a high five and a brotherly hug be too cheesy?

My first day's cycling started off with no one to share the moment and under a hot, midday sun. With half the day already gone, I was in a hurry to start. There was no ceremony. The streets of Vila Real were thick with tourists, too crowded to cycle through. I pushed my bike to the route's starting point by the ferry terminal, touched the sign that marked the route, swung my leg over the crossbar, and pushed off down the paved Avenida da República, turning right where the river met the sea and heading towards Monte Gordo.

Despite the heat and all the other problems of the day, my stress soon lifted, and I began to enjoy the ride. A bike will do this to your mood. I wonder how many millions could be saved from health budgets if doctors prescribed bike rides, rather than anti-depressant drugs. Travelling at speed, I created my own breeze and felt truly relaxed for the first time in two days.

Two years later, at this very point (less than one kilometre into our journey), Iain cycled alongside me with a huge smile on his face and shouted, "Hey, if it all goes as well as it has so far, we should do this every year!" It wouldn't be too long before he was screaming at me as we cycled along a busy dual carriageway in the pitch dark, "Nobody is enjoying this!"

Two kinds of tourists visit Monte Gordo. In the summer months, the resort is packed with mobility scooter-riding pensioners, attracted by the flat terrain and full English breakfast cafes. Out of season, it is a popular base for elite athletes who attend winter training camps hosted in the resort's larger hotels.

I was pondering which group I would be more at home with when my body violently let me know. My stomach cramped. This was a real emergency. I quickly pulled up outside the Yellow Praia Monte Gordo Hotel and rushed inside to find a toilet. Shit (diarrhoea, to be precise), could my day get any worse?

Knowing that my ride was going to take me out into the open countryside, miles from the nearest porcelain pot, I knew I could be in trouble. In a panic, I helped myself to a fresh roll of paper from the hotel restroom. If I was going to be caught short in the wilderness, I sure as hell wasn't going to wipe my arse on a cactus. Dressed exclusively in Lycra, I had nowhere to hide my newly-liberated toilet roll and decided to stroll back out through the large hotel lobby with the paper in plain sight. I looked like a desperate man. Nobody was going to stop me.

Back on my bike, I concentrated somewhat nervously on putting the miles in. Post-diarrhoea explosion (thank God it never came back), I felt a lot lighter and whizzed through the countryside. However, in my rush to escape with my stolen toilet roll, I had forgotten to put my cycling gloves back on. Usually, this wouldn't have been a problem but under the intense Portuguese sun, things were very different.

The first leg of the Ecovia has to be my favourite. If you don't have the time or the stamina to complete the entire route, I suggest the ride from Vila Real to Tavira, which has a little bit of the whole Algarve experience.

Over the 21 km that sandwich Vila Real and Tavira, you'll ride through bustling seaside resorts (such as Monte Gordo and Altura), pine forests, and citrus groves, past beautiful coastal villages (such as Cacela Velha) and manicured golf courses, over rickety bridges, and into the alien landscapes of the Ria Formosa's salt pans. The cycle path seems to change every couple of kilometres, from smooth asphalt to rough stone and everything in between. If you're not in a hurry, take your time, and remember – you're on holiday.

During a family holiday on this section of the ride, I once came across a travelling circus. Unlike the UK, Portuguese circuses still employ animal acts and travel with a wide range of exotic animals (if you are an animal lover, you might want to avoid them). Cycling past the big top, I came face-to-face with a large cage, housing a tethered elephant, camel, and lion. They didn't look too happy in their cramped conditions, and I wanted to take a quick photo to show my daughters why I believe circuses shouldn't use animal acts. Unfortunately, I hadn't charged my smartphone before the ride, and my battery had died. Upon returning home, Rose asked me if I had seen anything interesting on my ride. "Sure," I replied, "an elephant, a camel, and a lion at the beach in Monte Gordo." Rolling her eyes in disbelief, this may have been the moment that she transitioned from the young girl who'd idolised her father into the cynical almost-teenager who knew that her dad was one of the most uncool people alive (it happens to us all).

With such a late start, I didn't have time to hang about and look for wildlife on this ride. If I did, I might have spotted what was happening to my gloveless hands.

I suffer from a skin condition called Vitiligo. Vitiligo is an autoimmune disorder that attacks the pigment in your skin, leaving white blotches across your body (typically on the hands, feet, and throat, and around the eyes and groin). On a white-skinned person living in northern Europe like me, Vitiligo mostly goes unnoticed. On a dark-skinned person, the condition can appear to be quite shocking. Vitiligo (along with some pretty major plastic surgery) is what turned Michael Jackson from a cute black kid into a scary-looking white guy. Vitiligo and the hot Portuguese sun are not a good combination. In just a couple of hours, my gloveless hands had turned from pure white to violent red and started blistering. This was going to hurt.

In an exercise akin to shutting the stable door after the horse has bolted, I quickly bought some children's complete sunblock and smothered myself in it. Later in the day, I caught a glimpse of myself in a mirror. Rather than the healthy glow I'd been hoping for, I resembled a frostbitten Arctic explorer – bright red with skin peeling from my face.

Update: *The local municipality has big plans for Monte Gordo, recently launching a 200-million-euro redevelopment project, which will see improvements to the seafront area and the addition of six new hotels to the resort. As with any big redevelopment project, this has divided local opinion. Some would suggest that, as one of the oldest resorts on the Algarve, it is long overdue for a facelift. Others would argue that turning Monte Gordo into a "mega-resort" like Vilamoura would ruin the area. Personally speaking, I can see both sides of the argument, but I am optimistic for the future of the region. By the time this book is published, I'll guess we'll have a good idea what the new Monte Gordo looks like.*

The Big Storm

While I don't need too much persuasion to stuff my panniers and jump on a flight to Portugal, persuading friends who haven't yet discovered their inner cyclist (there's one in all of us) can be a little challenging. As bizarre as it might sound, the idea of cycling several hundred kilometres in the baking heat doesn't appeal to some people – I know, it's crazy.

So, when my friend Dave suggested doing something for charity in 2018, I jumped right in with the idea of a bike ride in Portugal. Dave thought the ride might entail a nice, relaxing 30 km jaunt between two beach resorts or around a picturesque and perfectly-manicured golf course. It wasn't until our flights and hotels were booked that I alluded it would be a bit more than this.

I believed the extra kilometres could be quickly sold to Dave with the promise of endless sunshine, cool beach breezes, and an abundance of café stops. A month before the ride, I shared a long-term weather forecast with him, and this backed up my promises. However, a week before we flew out, everything had changed, and a solid weekend of rain was forecast.

Upon boarding the aircraft at Manchester Airport, one of the cabin crew spotted our panniers and bike helmets and told us we would be flying into one of the biggest storms Portugal had seen in years. Dave didn't look happy.

Upon landing in Faro, it didn't appear too bad – just the odd spot of rain here and there – but as we disembarked the aircraft, the same crewmember updated us on the status of the storm. Apparently, it would now hit the following day.

Between the four of us on the trip, we each consulted our smartphones and got four very different weather forecasts, ranging from blazing sunshine to catastrophic conditions.

We decided the best approach was to set off as early as possible in the morning and get some kilometres in before the storm hit, taking shelter along the route if needed.

The sun rose at 6.50 AM. We were in Monte Gordo by 7.10 AM. The rain started at 7.20 AM. The first flash of lightning filled the distant sky at 7.30 AM. We were going to get wet, but it looked like the worst of the storm was out to sea and would miss us.

Or so we thought.

As we pushed through the forest tracks between Monte Gordo and Retur and headed out on our first short stretch on the notorious N125 road, the rain really started coming down in torrents. The flashes of lightning seemed to be getting closer, until they were directly above us.

Suddenly, just as we were pulling into the town of Altura, there was a massive explosion in the sky that was just far too close for comfort.

Okay, I'll admit it: For some strange reason, I have an irrational fear of being struck by lightning. I think I must have seen a TV documentary about people who have survived lighting strikes and just assumed that one day, it would happen to me. Apparently, if you are ever in a thunderstorm and you can feel the hair on the back of your neck stand up, you could be in serious trouble, and you should curl up into a little ball with your head between your legs. Inevitably, whenever I hear a clap of thunder, the hairs on the back of my neck, arms, and everywhere else instantly stand to attention. Yes, I might be a coward, but the thought of sitting on a steel bike in the middle of an electrical storm in the wide open countryside wasn't helping that fear.

I could see way behind me that Chris was having trouble with his bike. It looked like his chain had come off, and he was crouched in now-torrential rain, trying to fix the problem.

As the lightning increased in ferocity, I was waiting for Iain or Dave to suggest we should go back to help him. Now, I'll be the first to admit that I'm usually a much better friend, but, as another bolt of lightning streaked across the sky (JESUS, THAT WAS CLOSE!), I figured there was no point creating a bigger, bike-shaped target for the lightning to strike. Iain and Dave obviously agreed, because they didn't look back either. I think, in our minds, we basically left Chris for dead. I wondered if, had he not caught up, we'd have gone back looking for him after the storm had passed, or if we'd have just denied any knowledge of his existence.

The storm wasn't something I was used to in this part of the world. Just six months earlier, on a family vacation, I remember taking refuge from the heat by climbing on a tiled fountain in Altura. I'd seek something a little drier and certainly less open to the elements this time around.

We ducked into the four-star Eurotel hotel, ordered the first of many rounds of bicas, and spent the next two hours dripping on their beautifully-polished floor while chatting with the mainly German clientele about the (thankfully, not literally) shocking weather.

We asked our incredibly helpful waiter if the weather was going to improve over the course of the weekend. Although he was delighted to chat, he told us he wasn't qualified to make such a judgement about the weather, and so, couldn't possibly comment. Perhaps his English-language skills relating to the weather didn't go beyond *scorchio*, or maybe he just didn't want to be the bearer of bad news.

Despite getting a soaking, we were all in good humour. Dave, in particular, was excited to see the footage of the storm he'd captured on his helmet-mounted Go-Pro camera. Sadly, he'd accidentally set the camera up to record time-lapse footage – thus missing every single lightning bolt and clap of thunder – so you'll just have to take my word for how terrifying it was.

One of the great things about going cycling on holiday – especially if you have a limited time to complete your journey – is that you've just got to get on with it. The weather might not always be to your liking, but it shouldn't stop you from doing what you initially set out to do. It may even add to the challenge, and, although making it more difficult at the time, will almost certainly create more memories for you. This definitely helps if you are writing a book about the experience.

As we sheltered from the worst of the storm, I looked at the other tourists in the hotel who had come to Portugal to relax by the pool or sit on the beach and felt a little sorry for them. In a few minutes, we would be cycling again and enjoying the ride regardless of the weather, while their plans for the day (and maybe even the whole weekend) had almost certainly been rained out.

The storm dispersed as quickly as it had arrived. In fact, the storm may have cleared much earlier than we initially thought, as, from the comfort of the hotel, we may have actually mistaken the sounds of passing aircraft flying along the coast to Faro for the sound of thunder. Hitting the road – and entirely wired from caffeine – we headed for the old fishing village (and my home away from home in Portugal), Cabanas de Tavira, where we would find our second breakfast for the morning.

Cabanas De Tavira

My family has holidayed in Cabanas for more than a decade now, and, as such, it's a place I feel very much at home in – perhaps even more so than I do in the UK.

Cabanas is just a place that thoroughly washes the stresses of modern living out of you. If you've not already fallen in love with life in the Algarve, I challenge you to visit this place and not succumb to its charms.

As holiday destinations go, it's not on most UK package holidaymakers' radars. However, it is incredibly popular with Spanish and Portuguese visitors who flock to the Algarve at weekends and for extended periods over the summer. It's also a popular destination for UK, Irish, and French investors who want to own a reasonably-priced (nothing is cheap) place in the sun with a little more authenticity than the more bustling resorts on the other side of Faro.

A typical day for me in Cabanas involves a trip to the beach, a light lunch, and a small beer at a roadside café (try the caracóis – snails cooked in garlic and oregano), then a quick dip in the pool to cool off before heading out to dinner at one of our favourite restaurants (the Sabores da Ria; D'Ines and Europa restaurants have my full endorsement). I like to close the day with a large whiskey and Coke for me, a huge gin and tonic for Sarah, and some mocktails for the kids, before settling down for some serious people-watching on the terrace outside Quasi's bar.

Once, while snacking on caracóis with my family (my daughters love them), we were approached by a perplexed Portuguese man. He apologised for being a little drunk (it was the weekend) before asking us if we could settle an argument he was having with a friend of his – a French gentleman who was equally inebriated. They had seen us enjoying the local delicacy and were confused that we were speaking English. He asked us where we were from, and we told him that we lived in England.

He thought about this for a moment and then said, "Ah, but you must come from the south of England." We replied that we actually came from the north of the country.

He shook his head, apologised again for being drunk, and told us that he had never seen an English child – particularly, one from the north – enjoying snails. As this was his favourite dish, it made him incredibly happy, and he shook all our hands rather vigorously before returning to his friend. For the next 20 minutes or so, every time we looked in the direction of the two friends, they smiled and waved, and occasionally, raised their glasses of beer in a toast. Who said the north of England didn't have any culture? …Okay, it was probably me.

The cycling opportunities in the neighbouring countryside, which I have often enjoyed with my family, are also fantastic, and I cannot imagine a holiday in the town without access to a bike.

When holidaying in Cabanas, I typically hire a cheap "beater" bike for the duration of my vacation from a local hire shop. These tend to be okay for trips to the supermarket or shorter rides along the coast. As we often stay in Cabanas for upwards of a month at a time, I'll negotiate a much cheaper rate for long-term hire. On my last visit, when returning the bike, the hire shop denied all knowledge of ever renting the bike to me in the first place. Perhaps I'm too honest – I insisted they take the bike back.

For the sake of my aching back and poor backside, if I'm planning any longer rides, I will arrange for MegaSport to deliver a much better-quality ride.

To the east of Cabanas is the incredibly pretty village of Cacela Velha. (In a perfect world,

I would be physically writing this book while sitting on the terrace of one of this tiny settlement's small cafés, instead of in a business unit on an industrial estate in Cleethorpes). If the rustic beauty of the village isn't enough for you, just wait until you catch sight of the beach. Seriously, the village has the most perfect view over a beach I have ever seen before (these are strong words for a man from Cleethorpes).

In the summer months, when the tide is high, a flotilla of small boats take people across from the little beach situated directly underneath the village to the main island beach. When the tide is slightly lower, beachgoers wade across the channel between the village and the beach with their beach umbrellas and towels raised above their heads. The sight reminds me of an army landing party storming a beach – without the guns, bullets, and associated carnage, of course.

For me, the peace and tranquillity of Cacela Velha perfectly sums up what is so appealing to me about the Eastern Algarve.

When visiting Cacela Velha, take a quiet moment to stroll respectfully (please, no photos) through the village's cemetery. There can perhaps be no better insight into a country's culture than viewing how they preserve the memory of their dead.

In 2018, as we explored the stacked tombs of the cemetery known locally as *gavetões* (which literally translates to "big drawer"), I could tell Iain was particularly shocked to see the coffins of many of the "residents" clearly visible inside. The guys gingerly tiptoed along the pathways between what essentially looked like oversized office filing cabinets for the dead, respectfully reading the dates, and matching names to the photographs displayed on the tombs. I know they were spooked, but I didn't realise just how much.

I left the guys in the cemetery to quickly make a phone call home when all of a sudden, there was a massive crash. The wind had blown a ceramic flowerpot balanced precariously on one of the graves to the ground, where it smashed to pieces. The shock of the sudden noise from amongst the quiet of the tombs sent my buddies running in fear. Chris actually let out a high-pitched scream. They tried to play it cool as they rapidly fled the cemetery, everyone pushing each other out of the way to secure their exit first, but I'd never seen them so keen to get back on their bikes and leave a place. As we cycled away, I saw Iain nervously looking back to make sure nobody (either alive or dead) was following us.

To the west of Cabanas is the charming town of Tavira. It's a lively but incredibly tasteful destination, packed with fantastic restaurants, cool bars, and a thriving arts scene. In the summer months, the town is taken over by artisan craft fairs and hugely popular outdoor live music, dance, and theatrical performances.

Be sure to cross the river and explore the winding streets, packed with bars, cafes, and restaurants, as well as craft shops and unique boutiques. Even the obligatory Irish pub, the Black Anchor, is worth a visit for good pub grub and its cool, riverside terrace. The pub is housed in a converted girls' school which could easily justify a TV restoration project series on Channel 4. While sitting by the water, take a close look at the river and its banks, and be prepared to marvel at just how much life the environment possesses. The river is literally crawling with life.

It's amazing what, and, occasionally, *who* you see in Tavira.

While strolling around Tavira one evening, I held a door open for a man whom I clearly knew but couldn't quite place. I greeted him with a cheery, "Hello, mate. Good to see you." He smiled and thanked me before walking off with his family.

"Who was that and how do I know him?" I asked Sarah. Sarah's used to me asking this question because I have a terrible memory for faces. Turns out it was the famous comedian, Jason Manford, whom we kept seeing popping up all over the place over the next few days. While it was clear many people like me also recognised him from the telly, he never appeared to get any hassle beyond the occasional shocked look of recognition from strangers which all celebrities must live with. I liked this; even TV stars need a little downtime, and I guess Tavira is the perfect place to find a little normality.

Tavira is regularly featured in the property press as the emerging hotspot for international investors to secure a holiday home in Portugal. Despite this attention, it retains its charm and has yet to be spoiled by mass tourism.

When cycling into Tavira, you'll come across the massive Tavira Gran-Plaza shopping mall. It's a big, ugly building which dominates the outskirts of the town. It's also a bit of an enigma to me. Aside from the always crazily busy Continente supermarket in the mall, the rest of the shops seem eerily quiet. With that said, there doesn't seem to be a high turnover of stores, so I guess they must be making money somewhere along the line. With a decent selection of shops, the mall is a great place to grab anything you might have forgotten to pack in your panniers. In 2014, I called in for a European two-pin socket phone charger. The mall also affords a great view from the rooftop food court terrace. The view is probably enhanced by the fact that you cannot see the mall itself.

Across from the mall is another building that is perhaps not as ugly but certainly more functional than beautiful. While the Restaurante Três Palmeiras might look like a truck stop, it offers some of the best grilled fish dishes the region has to offer. It's incredibly popular with locals and tourists alike and is exceptionally busy during lunchtime, when diners will happily stand in line, waiting for a table. Go for the fish; ignore the view.

With that said, the Gran-Plaza is but a blot on the landscape of what is a beautiful town well worth a visit. If you have limited time in Tavira, visit the town's Camera Obscura. Housed in an old water tower, the centuries-old technology gives you a virtual tour of the town. It's like an offline version of Google Earth powered by sunlight, rope pulleys, mirrors, and magnifying lenses.

If I was a local, I'm not so sure how I would feel about the ever-present lens of the Camera Obscura, sweeping across the city. On our first visit, our guide warned us that, occasionally, the tour included gratuitous nudity.

A word of warning when visiting Tavira: Be careful where you park your bike. I once saw an elderly lady (she was easily in her mid-90s) thrown into an absolute fit of rage upon finding two bikes leaning against her front door in one of the winding, café-lined streets. I'm kind of glad that my kids don't understand much Portuguese, because her language sounded biblical in its level of profanity. She then proceeded to pick each bike up and throw them several meters across the path and onto the ground. These weren't ultralight carbon models. They looked like they were made of solid steel scaffold poles.

She reminded me of an old lady who lived (and maybe still does) across the road from our first apartment in Cabanas. Every morning, while eating breakfast on the balcony, I would see this bent old lady who could have easily been more than 100 years old, climbing an almost-vertical outdoor staircase to her rooftop terrace to hang her washing. Year-in, year-out, the old lady would be there, defying the aging process and sending my blood pressure soaring as she teetered around at the top of the stairs. She would then slowly climb down from the roof and feed all the stray cats in the area that flocked to her front door. It's interesting to note that she didn't appear to be a lonely old lady; her family was constantly visiting and could have easily helped her with her chores.

I think she was just used to working hard. Perhaps it's what kept her going. We moved apartments a couple of years ago. I wouldn't be surprised if she's still scaling those stairs with her arms full of washing.

The moral of the story is: Don't mess with Portuguese pensioners. I don't know if it's the diet of fresh fish, the constant supply of vitamin D from the ordinarily ever-present sunshine, or the occasional (medicinal) small glass of port, but they're made of tough stuff down there.

I personally believe that Cacela Velha, Cabanas, and Tavira may have been able to retain their charm because their beaches are only accessible by boat. For some holidaymakers who perhaps want everything on their doorstep, this might be more trouble than it is worth. However, in the cases of these East Algarve treasures, they would be entirely wrong because the beaches in this area are amongst the best in the world. It's perhaps a cliché to describe them as "best-kept secrets", but I kind of like this status, so… shhh! Don't tell too many people.

The Power of Community

For as long as we have been visiting the region, a rickety, old, wooden bridge on the cycle route between Cabanas and Tavira has always been a point of fascination for my daughters.

Year after year, the bridge has become even more buckled and twisted, and every time we crossed the bridge on our bikes, my daughters would approach it with caution and ask, "Is it safe?" and, "What would happen if it fell down?"

I would joke, "We'll all die," before riding confidently over the creaking structure and then laughing at them while they gingerly pushed their bikes over, fearing imminent collapse.

Well, it turns out the bridge wasn't so safe after all, and, following years of neglect, was finally fenced off by the local authorities.

Lack of access to the bridge represented a small problem for the Pie Eaters in 2018 – meaning, we'd have to make a slight detour. This meant joining the N125 again and probably riding the road straight into Tavira. While this wouldn't have been a problem, I wanted to cycle to Tavira via the off-road route in the hope of catching sight of the region's famous pink flamingos in the region's equally famous saltpans.

I quickly jumped on a Facebook Group and solicited the collective wisdom of a group of local expats for their ideas around alternative routes. One suggestion was to climb over the barriers, which the locals apparently do. However, the thought of four fat blokes (sorry, three fat blokes and a ginger one) and their overloaded bikes putting too much strain on the already dangerously weak bridge plagued my mind.

Thankfully, another group member sent me an image of an updated map of the route, which only involved a slight detour along the N125 before re-joining the cycle route on the other side of the rickety bridge – the perfect solution.

I wondered what other problems the group could help me with. Thinking back to previous rides, our early morning starts meant that breakfast wasn't always available at our hotels. Who better to ask for suggestions for breakfast venues than the local expats? Suggestions flew in, along with several offers of home-cooked meals along the route, and other offers of support and help, should we need them. We also solicited a number of charitable donations from complete strangers. What can I say? Some people are really nice. I'm sure that, had we'd asked, we could have secured free accommodations for the ride, but I'm not sure I would wish the Portugal Pie Eaters on anyone as houseguests.

Snakes on a Bike

Despite my sunburn, I was happy to be making good time. I pushed on through Cabanas, past the Golden Club Cabanas Resort, and up onto the dirt tracks that separate Cabanas from Tavira.

Out of the corner of my eye, I was surprised to see a snake sticking its head out of the grass by the side of the path. This was something I'd never seen in Portugal before, but I didn't have time to stop and investigate further, so I pushed on. I was even more surprised when, just as I was passing the reptile, it slithered out at high speed from its hiding place and darted straight between my wheels.

I didn't see or feel any impact as my back wheel surely went over the creature's body, and, when I looked back, there was no sight or sound of the animal.

Thank God. I must have missed it.

As I was cycling up through Tavira, past the local police station, and with no time to stop for lunch, I felt my panniers first catch my rear wheel before being pulled into the spokes, causing me to stop abruptly and nearly sending me over the handlebars before falling back and crunching my groin on the crossbar. My bike was too big for me, but when I ordered the bikes, I didn't want to admit that my brother was taller than me, so I added a couple of inches to my height. This made getting on and off the thing very difficult, and slipping from my saddle wasn't ideal. I swore loudly, forcing the local constabulary to look in my direction and laugh at my predicament. I'm not sure what they shouted at me, but I'm sure it wasn't an offer of assistance. Little did I know, my roadside sideshow was going to get even more entertaining.

I pulled my (now slightly torn) panniers free from my spokes (which, thankfully, survived the trauma) and started to adjust the straps to make sure the bags wouldn't become entwined with the back wheel again. As my sunburnt fingers struggled with the straps, half the mutilated body of the (thankfully, dead) snake fell from the bottom of my panniers. I dropped the bike, jumped about three feet in the air, and performed what I can only describe as a contemporary dance piece.

I'll admit to also dropping some pretty colourful swear words. Still, nobody came to my assistance. The rest of the snake was glued by its baking guts to my panniers.

Why is it that you can never find a stick when you need one?

Fighting Crime

While most of the off-road sections of the Ecovia are car-free, this isn't always the case. Most of the cars rattling along the dirt tracks tend to be agricultural workers, and they are mostly happy to give cyclists plenty of room as they slowly pass by.

However, not everyone is so willing to share the road safely.

Occasionally, vehicles travelling at a ridiculous pace will throw huge clouds of dust into the faces of anyone unlucky to be in their path, pushing cyclists and pedestrians to the side of the road.

Okay, some of these careless drivers might just be idiots – you get them everywhere. However, the back roads and dirt tracks of the Algarve are also allegedly used by drug smugglers and other criminal gangs, hoping to avoid detection on the busier roads as they travel between resorts to ply their trade. Every time a car tears past me at breakneck speeds on these ordinarily placid paths, I wondered what their hurry might be.

This hasn't escaped the notice of the Portuguese police (GNR) who regularly patrol the back roads and dirt tracks of the Ecovia, often on horseback.

The first time I came across a police presence on this route was on a solo ride between Tavira and Fuseta. I came tearing down a hill and around a sharp corner to come face-to-face with two spectacular police horses, which stayed perfectly calm, despite the dust cloud I threw up as I hit the brakes. The horses towered above me like the scene from *Lord of the Rings* when the hobbits are hiding from the Black Riders.

Obviously noticing my panic, the mounted officers quickly reassured me with a smile and a friendly wave before slowly trotting on. They probably weren't looking for reckless cyclists.

I'm not a horse person, but I thought that riding horseback along the Ecovia might just be the second best way to explore the Algarve. If you could ignore the occasional tussle with a drug dealer or gun-wielding gang member, I'm sure this must be one of the most laid-back jobs on the planet. No wonder the officers looked so chilled out.

And if you are going for chilled out, this little stretch of the coast, which takes you past the incredibly serene settlements of Santa Luzia and Luz, definitely qualifies.

Fuseta – Not Such a "Relaxing" Place

Fuseta has a small but active fishing fleet, and the smell of fresh fish being grilled outside the town's restaurants almost draws you to the seafront. It's another of those sleepy fishing villages that you'll never tire of stumbling across when you're on the Algarve, and, as such, it's a great place to stop off for a beer (well, you need the carbs!). The place just seems to operate at a different pace than the rest of the world.

Most of us looking to escape the fast pace of modern living would think that this is a good thing, but Iain struggled with the laid-back attitude toward life that was adopted by some of the local population.

I'm sure Iain won't mind me sharing the fact that he can find it hard to "relax" – especially when he is away from the comforts of home. Perhaps it was the difference in the food or water, but as we pushed into Fuseta, Iain had a sudden urge to "relax", so we pulled up at a ramshackle beach bar and ordered three beers.

Iain quickly made his way to the facilities to find a group of fishermen sitting in the shade directly outside the door, which he struggled to open. The elderly chap nearest the door demonstrated how it was opened and secured with a length of rope. To keep the door shut once inside, you had to keep a tight hold of the rope. Iain was gone for a good 15 minutes before he re-joined myself and Euan. He looked flushed.

"I couldn't bloody go. There were no lights inside, and you had to hold a rope to keep the door shut. You could see the bloody old men sitting outside the door through the gaps in the wood. I could hear them laughing. They could hear me. I think they were watching."

Who knew what floated these old sea dogs' boats? But, I can guarantee that watching a fat, sweaty guy in mismatched Lycra taking a shit probably wasn't at the top of their list of niche interests. Then again, as anyone who has access to the Internet knows, there is a niche for everything these days.

We ordered another beer before pushing on to a more "relaxing" spot.

Lost in Time

Throughout this book, I mention the N125. The N125 is a road that runs along the entire length of the Algarve and once had the privilege of being known as the most dangerous road in Europe, frequently portrayed in the media as "the death road." Numerous members of our supportive friends on the Facebook Group who helped us out with the rickety bridge and breakfast offers had also warned us to stay well clear of the N125, which wasn't always possible.

Thankfully, a new motorway system, proactive policing, and zero-tolerance drink-driving laws (which many people in Portugal once argued were incompatible with Portuguese culture) have made the road a lot more forgiving towards cyclists. This doesn't mean you don't have to be careful – especially as you approach roundabouts and junctions.

I have to say, the vast majority of drivers we encountered on the N125, and all the other roads we rode in the Algarve, treated us with a tremendous amount of respect, giving us more than enough space and plenty of time to navigate some of the more complicated junctions. Give me the N125 over any busy road in the UK any day.

However, with its old reputation in mind, I wanted to spend as little time on the "dreaded" N125 as possible on my first ride. I've since come to think of the N125 as a trusted friend that can get you places a little faster (especially if you want to avoid some of the hills on the last stretch of the ride), but it took a real spooky incident to persuade me that perhaps the N125 wasn't so scary after all.

Heading towards Olhão from Fuseta, I was overtaken by two cyclists on mountain bikes whom I assumed were going in the same direction as me. I tucked in behind them in a vain attempt to prove my fitness. They were younger, fitter, and faster than me, and I struggled to keep up with them, eventually losing them in the middle of nowhere. It was then I realised that they were taking a completely different route, and I had completely lost the cycle path. (Remember – at the time, I didn't really have a usable map.) The scrub was cutting my calves to pieces. I was clearly lost. Where the hell was I?

Then, things started getting *really* strange.

The wind seemed to change direction, blowing dust everywhere. I felt a shiver as the temperature plummeted, despite the sun still being high in the sky. I was suddenly surrounded by hundreds of small brown goats. They appeared from out of nowhere, bleating loudly, with clanking bells tied around their necks. They were being herded by an equally brown gentleman of an undeterminable age. It wasn't just his skin tone that was brown; his hat, shirt, jacket, trousers, and boots were all the same colour of the scrubland his goats were grazing on. He almost looked like a sepia-toned photograph. As he walked past me, I asked him for directions. He turned and looked through me as if I didn't exist before continuing with his herd. Then, he was gone.

It felt like two time zones had suddenly merged, and I was witnessing life on the Algarve as it used to be 100 years ago. Was he a ghost?

It was then I decided to quit the wilderness and hit the N125, circumnavigating Olhão and heading straight into Faro.

A Broken Promise

For as long as I can remember, I have been lobbying my eldest daughter, Rose, to join me in riding the Ecovia. I figured a five-day ride might be an excellent opportunity for some father/daughter bonding.

At first, she was entirely against the idea. However, following some careful negotiation – which included a visit to a waterpark and dinner at the rather fancy Gastronomy Restaurant in Cabanas (expensive tastes, my daughter) – she bought into the idea. What made the ride even more attractive was that she might be able to procure a few extra days off school if she did the ride for charity.

I promised to use the 2018 ride to scope the ride out and make sure it really was suitable for a 14-year-old girl. Dave, being our token millennial, was the nearest thing to a teenage girl we had, and so, I was keen to see how he coped (which, as it turns out, was admirably). However, Dave will be the first to admit the ride was much harder than he thought it would be. This probably had something to do with the weather, and Portugal not being as flat as I'd promised. But I'm also sure that, had he actually got on a real bike in the weeks before the ride, he would have managed it a hell of a lot better.

Knowing that Rose wouldn't be too keen to put in the training miles, I started to think she might struggle also. Then, there was the problem of the N125. While I felt perfectly safe on the "death road," the sight of a 14-stone man in high-visibility cycle wear isn't too hard to miss. I wondered how safe a rider who was smaller and less confident in the saddle would feel.

Ultimately, it was the thought of dragging my daughter along the N125, and not Dave's "weakness", that made me reconsider the possibility of a father-and-daughter ride. Rose didn't take the news well.

I offered Rose the opportunity of doing the off-road sections of the Ecovia and jumping on the train for sections where we would typically have to ride the N125, but she wasn't interested, telling me it was "all or nothing". Bearing in mind her earlier thoughts of doing (or, to be more precise, *not* doing) the ride, this might have been a rather convenient excuse.

Although Rose has no memory of the event, she has actually already cycled a good chunk of the route, albeit as an infant in the child seat on the back of a bright purple ladies' shopping bike (the only bike available with a child seat for hire that day from a local shop in Cabanas). We cycled from Cabanas to Vila Real de Santo António and back to Monte Gordo (taking the train home), with Rose singing "Five Little Men in a Flying Saucer" the whole way.

It's not just the incredibly irritating song that stuck in my mind. We'd stopped at Cacela Velha, where we enjoyed a cool drink on the equally cool roof terrace of the Casa Azul before taking the steps down to the shore, where Sarah swam over to the island beach. We then cycled out to Vila Real de Santo António before doubling back to Monte Gordo, where Rose hung out with the son of a lady who tuned out to be a genuine Nashville country-and-western singer (complete with big hair, a faded denim jacket, and cowboy boots) and her Portuguese husband.

In many ways, Rose was part of the ride that made me fall in love with cycling in the region. Maybe when she is slightly older, we'll get the opportunity to reconnect with the ride together.

Update: *The Gastronomy Restaurant is no more. I guess when the food is as good as it already is in Cabanas, fancy doesn't really cut it.*

Ola Olhão

Subsequent trips later, we've never had a problem finding Olhão (via the N125, d'oh!) and have always stopped for a couple of beers and the obligatory tosta mista by the town's impressive red-brick fish, fruit, vegetable, and meat markets. If supermarket shopping has left you a little detached from your food, a visit to these two market buildings will be something of a culture shock. Be prepared to be pushed out of the way by overly aggressive old ladies (I told you, they are tough!) fighting over fish you've never heard of before and cuts of meat that might turn more sensitive stomachs (nothing is wasted here).

The permanent market buildings are supplemented by a large outdoor market on Saturdays, selling everything from the usual tourist tat to locally-produced agricultural produce, including cages of live chickens and rabbits. I often wonder how many expats stand in line in the hopes of acquiring a new pet behind locals who are buying these animals for the pot. I also wonder if the price of a pet chicken is a lot more expensive than one destined to be turned into spatchcocked frango.

If mountains of meat and fish or caged livestock aren't your thing, or you haven't got the space in your panniers for anymore tourist tat (a great excuse us cyclists have not to buy anything), Olhão has some of the most impressive graffiti and street art I have ever seen. Like most cities, graffiti was once frowned upon, and the artists were regularly locked up, but in recent years, Olhão has come to embrace it as art, and much of it is not only tolerated, but actually commissioned by the local council. I personally love it. Cycling in Olhão is like cycling into a huge, outdoor art gallery.

However, the graffiti isn't to everyone's tastes. A quick search on the forums of TripAdvisor regarding Olhão reveals the kind of moral outrage generally reserved for the pages of *The Daily Mail*.

On a universally positive note, I'm told that Olhão's two main beaches, the Ilha da Culatra and Ilha da Armona (which can be reached by boat), are off-the-scale and definitely at the top of my "must-do" list for a future visit.

With my friends in tow in 2014, the 9 km from Olhão to Faro was a breeze, but the first time around, I was struggling.

Le Bonk

It was getting late in the day, I was sunburnt, I was hungry, and I was on a road I didn't want to be on. I was getting depressed. At the time, I didn't realise I was suffering from a cycling malady known as "le bonk."

A bonk might sound like a lot of fun. It's not. It's the cycling equivalent of "the wall" that long-distance runners hit during marathons. It saps your energy, destroys your morale, and sends your mind to very dark places. At the time, I didn't know that the best cure for a bonk was as easy as having something to eat. I pulled over to the side of the road and phoned Sarah, literally bursting into tears when she answered.

After being told to pull myself together and enjoy my "little cycling holiday," I reached into my panniers, then pulled out and consumed an overly ripe and completely squashed banana and a handful of Jelly Babies. Two minutes later, I was back in the saddle and singing away to myself, happier than I'd been all day, as I headed along the busy road into Faro.

Funny things, bonks. Easy come, easy go.

I can thank my lack of navigational skills for taking me into the city via a route I was unfamiliar with. I rode past high-rise housing estates, office blocks, university and hospital buildings, and was undoubtedly a long way from the tourist trail. Spotting some friendly-looking pedestrians, I stopped to ask directions.

Two men (one large, one small) dressed in ill-fitting suits (one too large, one too small – perhaps they should have swapped) were more than keen to help, despite their lack of English and my non-existent Portuguese. At one point, all three of us gathered around a patch of dirt while one of the men carved a rudimentary map into the dust with a small stone. The men argued and took turns deleting routes with their smartly-polished, soon-to-be-dusty shoes. My cycle ride had suddenly taken on the importance of a military operation, and my two new friends weren't going to leave anyone behind. I shook their hands and thanked them with big smiles, thumbs-up, and multiple expressions of *"Obrigado",* and then cycled off, none the wiser to where I was going.

By the time I reached my hotel, I was ready for another bonk. I found relief in a Big Mac meal with a small beer instead of a Coke, and promptly hit the hay.

Throughout the 2012 ride, I endured far too many prolonged bonks. Believing I was doing myself some good by burning a few much-needed calories, I now know that cycling is as much about fuelling your ride as it is about pushing pedals, and this is just one of the reasons why cycling is such a pleasurable pastime. Would I have enjoyed my ride in 2012 more without the self-inflicted bouts of mind-blowing, hunger-induced depression? Quite possibly.

It wasn't just me who struggled to reach Faro. In 2018, Dave also had some difficulties.

The Best 99p A Cyclist Can Spend

I'm a bit of a worrier. In fact, worrying is a bit of a hobby of mine. In fact, if I don't have anything to worry about, I'll worry about that. Naturally, the prospect of a long-distance bike ride will throw up lots of scenarios I can worry about. Perhaps this is why I'm so keen to tackle such big rides.

I've often wondered what would happen if my bike chain broke while I was on one of my longer rides. Would I be able to fix it?

Thankfully, this has never happened to me. Yes, I've suffered multiple punctures, the occasional broken spoke, and, once, I even lost a pedal, but my chain has always remained in one piece.

But that doesn't stop me from worrying about it. Well, I guess the worst thing that could happen is an expensive taxi ride home, but if you're anything like me, you'll probably want to be a little more self-sufficient than that.

So, before the 2018 ride, I picked up a little gizmo called an SRAM Powerlink. Essentially, this is a quick fix solution to a potentially catastrophic problem. The little link only set me back a cool 99p, and I'll tell you what; it was the best 99p I have ever spent.

We were perhaps 7 km from home on the first day of the ride, just coming into Faro up a slight incline on a jam-packed section of the N125, when Dave suddenly disappeared from view. We waited for him for a few minutes at the next junction before a local cyclist sped past us and shouted back that Dave's chain had broken.

Initially, I thought perhaps that this was lost in translation, and his chain had simply come off, but as we pushed our bikes back along the hard shoulder to find him, there he was with a snapped chain.

Okay, this wasn't exactly a catastrophe. Dave could have very easily walked his bike into Faro, but I was conscious of this being his first long-distance bike ride, and I didn't want his first day in the saddle to end on a sour note.

Now, I'd never used the chain attachment on my trusty multi-tool in anger before, but I couldn't believe how easy it was to make the repair. I think the hardest part was working out how to thread the chain back on and around the jockey wheels while the bike was upside-down. We were back on the road within five minutes.

This 99p gizmo got us back to the hotel, where we were able to replace the chain (actually, MegaSport came out first thing in the morning and replaced the entire bike at no extra cost and with only a 30-minute delay to our schedule). The great thing is, the Powerlink is entirely reusable if a chain should ever break again, ready to save another adventure.

I don't expect to see too many broken chains in my life, but you can bet that little chain link will ride with me wherever I go.

It should be noted that I don't believe Dave's mechanical problem was in any way caused by the quality of the bike he was riding. Over the years, we've suffered from many mechanical issues. It's just a fact of life on the road. Burst tyres, snapped spokes, and even broken chains happen to all long-distance cyclists – especially when bikes are being ridden hard by overweight guys through difficult conditions. Some of the wet gravel roads we were riding did not provide optimal conditions, and I'm sure all our drive chains and gears were suffering. The great thing about the simplicity of bikes is that, with just a little bit of knowledge, a few simple tools, and the occasional hack, you can generally be back on the road again within a few minutes.

We were, of course, secure in our knowledge that if anything went wrong with the bikes beyond our (limited) mechanical skills, the team at MegaSport would soon come to our rescue in their big, green van. Realistically, there was very little chance of the ride failing in the first two days. The abundance of accommodation on the Algarve and the relatively short distances (50 miles) between planned stops would mean that any unplanned overnight stops could easily be made up on the following day's cycle. It would be a different story if something went wrong on Day Three of the ride, with limited time to get to the end and back again to make the train back to Faro, but we weren't going to worry about that now.

Stop Press: *The local government is apparently planning to complete the off-road section of the Ecovia between Olhão and Faro, meaning that cyclists should be able to avoid some of the busiest sections of the N125. Local press reports suggest that the work, which is part of a considerable rejuvenation program in Olhão, will start in 2019.*

Escaping Faro

Faro offers visitors so much more than a drop-off point for the Algarve's famous beaches and golf courses. The city offers some excellent shopping, dining, and sophisticated night spots. While I cannot speak for any of my friends, I would certainly not describe myself as particularly sophisticated, but despite this, we certainly found ourselves quite at home in the old port.

Now, I'd visited Faro plenty of times before, and, as I am really fond of the city, I wanted to show it off to my friends.

I think Faro is a really cool city. I'm sure the local people – particularly the young people who are currently reinventing the urban environment – already know this. The rest of the world will undoubtedly catch on sooner, rather than later. In ten years' time, I wonder if Faro will have evolved from a city that serves the Algarve to the beating heart of the region itself.

One of the things I really like about the city is its fading charm. Large areas of the city – particularly those near the train station – are in various states of disrepair. In many ways, it reminds me of Budapest – a city I lived in for five years following the collapse of communism at the turn of the century. Every derelict building and dishevelled façade seems to scream "opportunity" to me.

In 2014, I primarily wanted to show them the famous Capela de Ossos, or "Bone Chapel" (as the name suggests, it is a church built out of human bones). Above the door to the chapel reads the inscription: *Stop here and think of the fate that will befall you*. Perhaps this would have served as a warning for the following day's cycling – only, I couldn't find the damn place. I swear to God, someone had moved it. Instead, we grabbed something to eat in Old Town (worth a walk around) and then went looking for a drink.

We did eventually find the Bone Chapel in 2018 – again, thanks to the GPS on my smartphone. What did we ever do without them? "Get lost" is the most obvious answer.

Had we not been delayed in 2018 by the weather and Dave's mechanical problems, I would have also liked to have taken the ferry to Faro Beach. While the beach at Faro isn't as spectacular as those in Cabanas or Tavira, it has a pretty cool vibe and is home to some really chilled-out beach cafes and bars. There is nothing pretentious about Faro Beach, which is probably why I like it so much. It's just a place where the locals go to catch the sun and relax, and that's good enough for me. While it is possible to reach the beach by bike, the ferry journey directly under the flight path into Faro Airport is absolutely breath-taking – particularly, at sunset.

Before dinner, we took the elevator up to the rooftop terrace bar of the Hotel Faro. This is a seriously cool venue with a view over the rooftops of the city, the city's small marina, and the airport. Situated directly in front of the hotel was a large stork's nest balanced carefully on top of a streetlight. How the hell these amazing structures stay secure in anything stronger than a gentle breeze is beyond me. I cannot even begin to imagine how these fantastic birds start to build these things. They are apparently very successful at doing so, because they are a ubiquitous sight all across the Algarve in both rural and urban areas.

It's worth mentioning that the quality of the dining experience in Faro can vary. This will have to change if the city is ever to attain a universally-accepted "cool" status. There are numerous smart-looking restaurants with equally smart-talking waiters who will lure you into what are mostly tourist traps where the food and the quality of the services don't always match the sales pitch. With that said, there are also many great, less-obvious places waiting for your custom. Therefore, it is perhaps best to check reviews or speak to a trusted local first if you want to guarantee your meal out in Faro will be memorable for all the right reasons.

In 2014, thanks to the recommendation of our hotel receptionist, we found a great little restaurant. Actually, they were *two* great little restaurants, with the smoking and non-smoking sections of the establishment housed in two separate commercial units. The food was authentically Portuguese, the service friendly and attentive, and most of our fellow diners were locals. Sadly, I have no idea what this restaurant was called, and, despite hours of research on Google, I have been unable to relocate it since. (Mind you, in 2014, I'm not sure we ever really knew where we were.)

I won't talk too much about our meals out in Faro in 2018, other than that on our first visit, Iain, Chris, and Dave opted for the same dish, which resembled a poorly-constructed children's meal in a "kids eat free" pub back home. Not good. On our second visit (on the last night), after complaining about a range of issues (food not arriving, wrong food arriving, poor quality food arriving), we actually left without paying. It's also interesting to note that the only meal they *did* get right was not on the menu. I asked if they could rustle me up my favourite Portuguese dish of black pork and clams, which they did to near perfection. Apparently, the chef had the skills to turn their hand to produce a reasonably decent meal; they were probably just bored to tears with the same old tourist menus they were forced to cook every night.

We did, however, find a great bar to end the night in, which we made good use of on both trips.

The Columbus Cocktail and Wine Bar, situated just across from Faro Marina, provided the perfect spot to soothe our aching limbs (and guarantee an aching head the next morning). Looking around the bar's crowded terrace, the Columbus was clearly very popular with a young, trendy crowd (which we didn't quite fit in with). Despite this, we were welcomed with open arms. This is perhaps because we were the only people drinking. I swear, there were at least 12 hipsters sitting across from us, and only one glass on the table.

Come the wee hours, the bar operates a 24-hour service. We were presented with a button that we were assured would bring a waiter straight to our table. It was too much fun to resist pressing it and ordering another round, and another round, and maybe one more.

We hit the hay at 3 AM with an alarm set for 7 AM. Perhaps this was the cause of our terrible confusion as we tried to escape the confines of Faro with all the success of Patrick McGoohan in an episode of "The Prisoner".

We have always stayed at the two-star Hotel Sol Algarve in Faro, primarily for its location and secure underground parking. Don't let the lack of stars put you off. The hotel is clean, and the staff are super friendly. Upon checking in in 2018, the receptionist actually remembered Iain and me from our previous visit in 2014. We must have created quite an impression. I'm not sure if this was a good thing or a bad thing. It might have had something to do with our visit to the aforementioned Columbus Cocktail Bar, and our trigger-happy fingers on the drinks button.

Escaping Faro is the one thing I always worry about when planning these rides. Seriously, I get anxiety about it for weeks before a ride and spend hours staring at the same roads on Google Maps, looking for the perfect route out of the city. For me, it's never been a simple process, and the rides in 2012, 2014, and 2018 all had their challenges at the start of the second day.

The Second Financial Crisis

I don't want to lead you on any further – my first ride across the Algarve failed on the second day. Don't judge me.

I started the morning with a good breakfast, loading up on carbs for the day's cycling ahead. The plan was to make an early start and pick up the cash Sarah had sent me via a Western Union office along the way.

The clerk at the Cleethorpes post office back home had a very different idea. She somehow persuaded Sarah to send me the money via a service called MoneyGram instead. She told Sarah that they offered the same service as Western Union, and I would have no problem picking up my emergency cash.

The clerk had apparently never been stranded alone in a foreign country with no money. Had she known how crucial it was that the funds reached me in good time, she would have done a little research to back up her confidence in the service. If she had, she would have known how many MoneyGram agents were open in Faro at the weekend at the time (two), and how their limited weekend operation would set me back by half a day before I could set off again under the midday sun.

The sign on the door said the office would open at 10 AM – although it was closer to 11 AM when someone actually saw fit to show up and find me standing nervously outside. I kept saying to myself that I would give them another 15 minutes, but the lack of funds kept me desperately frozen to the spot. It took another 15 minutes for the clerk to turn on her computer, log in, and figure out how to work the photocopier to make a copy of my passport. Despite the delay, the transaction itself was swift and painless, and I soon felt like I had more money that I knew what to do with.

I'm not proud of what I did with my newfound wealth.

I pushed off with very little motivation to actually cycle to my destination. Within minutes of joining the Ecovia again, I'd taken a wrong turn and ended up at the airport. I doubled back and tried again, only to end up at the airport again.

The third time, I luckily managed to get a little further along the track – only to be greeted by a high wire fence, guarding a half-finished construction site. Apparently, there was no way around.

I persuaded myself (with minimal internal argument) that it was probably not a good idea to set off on another full day of cycling under the heat of the midday sun. Instead, I cycled back to the train station and pushed my overloaded bike onto the next train to Portimão, and then cycled the short distance to my hotel in Praia da Rocha, where I would resume my ride the following day.

Was I disappointed in myself?

Yes.

Did I care?

At the time, yes and no – but upon reflection, yes. I was gutted.

While I concede this was a colossal failure on my behalf, the day in Praia de Rocha wasn't wasted. The high-rise resort actually boasts some of the best beaches in Europe, and I enjoyed a leisurely cycle along the coast towards the beautiful coastal area around Alvor.

However, I was so disheartened by my failure – notably, when my kids presented me with a homemade "well done" card upon my return home – that I vowed to return to the Algarve and complete the missing part of the tour at the earliest opportunity. I did this the following year in August, during a family holiday.

Despite taking the earliest possible train to Faro, the sun quickly rose in the sky, and before I knew it, it was 40 degrees. Despite the oven-like temperatures almost killing me, I loved every red-hot minute of the ride and was incredibly proud to say that I'd finally cycled the entire route – even if it did take me more than a year.

Many things stick out in my memory about that ride:

1. Stopping every five minutes to check my route out of Faro. I'd printed out several pages of Google Maps with the route carefully mapped out in highlighter pen, which I would then compare to *another* Google Map on my smartphone, highlighting my current position via GPS. I've told you before, I'm not very good with maps, and the constant stops to make sure that I wasn't straying from the route took up an inordinate amount of time. I hate to think what the constant pauses did to my split times. Everyone knows someone who can describe a journey in intricate detail by road numbers and the

specific junctions they passed through. I'm not that person.

2. Dragging my bike along the sand at Quarteira after somehow taking the wrong route into town and ending up on the beach. You don't realise how heavy your bike is until you are forced to drag it through incredibly fine sand.

3. Lying down in the middle of the street in Albufeira and drinking three cans of Fanta in quick succession while suffering from what I thought might be the initial stages of heat exhaustion. Albufeira was incredibly busy. In fact, it was too busy to cycle through, meaning that I was forced to push my bike up the hill and out of town (or, at least, that's my excuse).

4. Pouring water over my head every time I stopped to hydrate myself. I often tell people that cycling in the heat isn't a problem, because you create your own cool breeze. This isn't true when the temperature climbs above 40 degrees centigrade. At these temperatures, even the breeze is too hot.

5. The fantastic, life-affirming, ice-cold glass of Sagres beer I rewarded myself with

upon arriving at Portimão. I stopped at the first bar I saw after crossing the river into town. Nobody said I had to cycle to the town's centre to validate my ride as complete. Passing the city limits sign was good enough for me.

6. Upon returning home, Sarah commented on how long the train journey back to Cabanas took. "I didn't think it was so far away," she said. Damn right, it's a long way away. I'm not in the habit of taking of taking little leisurely rides; I'm bloody hardcore, me.

7. Being persuaded to go out for dinner upon returning to Cabanas (despite just wanting to go to bed). I ordered chicken on the stone for my evening meal and was presented with a plate of raw chicken meat and a red-hot stone to cook it on (perfect on such a hot day). Probably breaking every food hygiene law, the waiter thought it would be a good idea to provide me with just one set of cutlery to cook and eat the chicken with. Well, what's a holiday without a dose of salmonella? The waiters also presented me with a bib to wear while cooking and eating my meal (this would become a theme on further adventures).

My kids thought it was hilarious. I was too exhausted to protest.

8. The best night's sleep I have ever had (thank God for air conditioning).

9. Not feeling *too* guilty about not leaving the pool area of our apartment the following day. (If I remember correctly, I may have even not pulled myself up from my sun lounger.)

The Blind Leading the Blind

Okay, I might be a doer, and I'm more than happy to initiate all manner of misadventures, but I'm equally happy to kick back and let someone else take charge. This is especially true when maps are involved, and the other person looks like they might know what they are doing.

I'd never met Euan before, but my good friend, Iain – whom I'd known since college – said he was a good guy, and that I'd like him. I did, and even after the following experience, I still do.

Iain had told me that Euan was incredibly well-travelled. In fact, if I can remember correctly, he told me that he was a bit of an adventurer. There was talk of climbing Kilimanjaro and cycling across the Alps.

Surely, this meant he'd be good with maps, and, based on my previous experience of trying to escape Faro, this would definitely be an advantage.

I think the fact that Euan had taken his own clipless pedals down to Portugal and wore cycling gear that didn't look like it had been purchased from Aldi lulled me into a false sense of security. This guy clearly knew what he was doing. I left Euan in charge.

Within just a couple of minutes of re-joining the Ecovia route in Faro, we arrived at the airport, doubled back, and found the same wire fence that had blocked my previous journey. This time, we circumnavigated the fence by pushing our bikes along a train track and over a bridge. Then, we proceeded to get thoroughly lost.

The thing is, Euan didn't seem so interested in checking the (rudimentary) maps we were carrying. He seemed to be relying on some inbuilt navigational aid. But, Euan was no homing pigeon, and his instinctive sense of direction was obviously completely broken. Stupidly, and despite the fact I'd successfully – if not rather slowly and methodically – followed the correct route on my solo rerun of the route the year before, I didn't question his apparent authority.

Euan took us into some dense woodland along a series of incredibly sandy paths, which made cycling virtually impossible. Along the way, we were chased by a "rabid" dog, which we tried to put off our scent with a packet of Jelly Babies. Then, we found our way into a large compound used to store hire cars and woke up the "friendly" security guard. He was very obviously drunk (he could barely stand) and quite surly, and what we initially assumed was a bottle in a brown paper bag turned out to be a somewhat rusty pistol. Thankfully, he was happy to give us directions instead of shooting us and sent us through a maze of salt plans and deep muddy ditches straight back to Faro Airport (albeit at the other end of the runway).

Three hours on the road, and we had virtually arrived back at the point we'd started from.

Along the way, Euan somehow broke two spokes – which, thankfully, didn't pull his wheel out of shape. He was able to replace them later with a couple of FibreFix emergency spokes which – like the Powerlink that saved Dave's ride in 2018 – I'd carried with me out of paranoia more than anything else. (I swear to God, I bring these things upon myself. If I'd packed a fire extinguisher in my panniers, someone's bike would have inevitably burst into flames.)

It was at this point that I retook charge. I abandoned the map and adopted the basic rule of navigation on the Algarve: If you can see the sea, and it's on your left-hand side, you're going in the right direction.

Somehow, this got us to the high-class resort town of Vilamoura in time for lunch.

Quick Sand

2018 was going to be the year we cracked Faro. We were armed with the BikeGPX app and couldn't get lost. Despite taking a new, unfamiliar route around the airport, we stayed on track and didn't get lost once. The only problem was that the ground was wet. In fact, it was *really* wet, and, in places, it sucked our tyres into the quagmire, making our progress incredibly slow.

Occasionally, a group of mountain bikers would speed past us, sending mud flying in our faces. We couldn't quite work out what their secret was. Somewhat frustratingly, they all appeared to be much older than us. How had they gotten so fit?

Then, one stopped to say, "Hello." He was on an eBike. Everything made sense now. Dave looked at his machine somewhat enviously.

Now, I don't know how you feel about eBikes, but I am always pleased to see older or less-able riders on them. In my mind, a bike gives you the most enormous sense of freedom you could ever hope for outside of childhood. Why would you deny anyone this? I would also like to think that an eBike may one day extend my riding life – hopefully, long into my dotage. It's also worth remembering that the more people who ride bikes (with or without a motor), the more visible we become as road users, and, therefore, the safer cycling becomes. eBikes are definitely a good thing.

It took us a long time to circumnavigate the airport. Part of this was due to the mud, but Iain can also take some of the blame for our slow progress, because he wanted to stop and film every aircraft that took off or landed as we made our way around the parameter fence. He told us that his son would love seeing the videos, but judging by the size of the smile on his face, it was Iain who was the aviation enthusiast.

Death by Golf

While I would struggle to dislike any region of the Algarve, the middle section of the route – Faro to Portimão – is perhaps my least favourite leg of the ride.

While the coast is universally beautiful, some of the more developed areas are just a bit *too* developed – some of it very tastefully, some of it not so much for my liking.

Don't get me wrong. It's very nice to cycle along the perfectly-manicured golf courses surrounding the high-end resort of Quinta do Lago, and there are some fantastic properties along this stretch of the Algarve that wouldn't look out of place in Beverly Hills. It's just a little *too* perfect, a little *too* manicured, and, in my rather humble opinion, utterly devoid of character.

As we cycled past the acres of golfing real estate, I couldn't help but feel that those who played the game would do themselves a lot more good if they walked between shots and didn't jump straight into a golf buggy and drive off. Mark Twain once said, *"Golf is a good walk spoiled."* It's not even that anymore. For an outdoor pursuit – certainly here on the Algarve – there are a lot of very fat people who play golf. Mind you, as a founding member of the Portugal Pie Eaters (pot, kettle) – well, you get the picture.

Okay, maybe I'm being unfair. The best plate of grilled sardines I have ever had in my life was almost certainly consumed in Vilamoura. The beach to the west of the resort is an excellent place for a long, seaside walk, with some cool and utterly unpretentious beach bars along the route to chill out and relax in. I have also enjoyed many an hour enviously eyeing up the yachts in the marina. However, I do wonder if the resort gets more generic every year, losing any of the limited, authentic Portuguese charm it may have once possessed. This is a shame, because I believe it is possible to be both authentic and luxurious at the same time.

It also should be said that the town of Quarteira (which adjoins Vilamoura) has undergone some much-needed redevelopment in recent years. The promenade is particularly pleasant – although, due to the sheer number of people who use the resort throughout the year, it can be challenging to navigate on a bike.

Whenever I think of Quarteira, I'm reminded of a holiday we took in the area before we were blessed with children and a family-owned apartment in Cabanas (they were the best of times; they were the worst of times). It was January, and our off-season flight to Portugal was packed with pensioners hoping for a little winter sun. I'm not exaggerating, but it took absolutely ages to board the aircraft, as so many passengers required assistance.

As we checked in for our flight, there was a little old lady in the queue to the front of us who walked with frame and seemed to be struggling with every step. She wore a big, woollen hat and a thick, quilted jacket. Despite this, she still looked cold. (Manchester in the winter is no place for the old.)

Two days later, as we strolled down Quarteira promenade, we caught sight of the same old lady. The walking frame had gone, she was wearing a tiny pair of shorts and a spaghetti-strap top, and, if I'm being completely honest, she looked so sprightly that I wouldn't have been surprised if she suddenly pulled a cartwheel. What a transformation! She was either cheating on her benefits back home or the Portuguese sea air had worked wonders on her health. I'm no cynic; I like to think it was the latter.

I particularly like Quarteira's little fish market and the surrounding area, which retains what I imagine to be some real, authentic Portuguese charm. It's also home to some pretty solid-looking seafood restaurants. Just across the road from the fish market, there is a little apartment with a green balcony. I don't know why, because I've never seen inside the building, but I've often thought that this would be my ideal holiday home, with just the right mix of resort and real-world urban sprawl. If you own this apartment and ever feel like selling, you know where to find me.

As we move along the coast, things start to liven up that little bit more. Heading in the direction of Albufeira and Praia da Rocha – well, we'll get on to those "good time" places in good time.

Breakfast in Vilamoura

Vilamoura, with its marina full of millionaires' super-yachts, seemed like a great place to stop for breakfast. Who knew that millionaires liked their good, old full-English breakfasts so much? There is, indeed, plenty of choice if you want a fry-up after parking your vessel.

After spending several hours in the wilderness – thanks in part to Euan's terrible navigation skills and my laissez-faire attitude to map reading – we were famished. In fact, it may even be fair to suggest that some of us (Iain) were bordering on *hangry*.

It should be pointed out that, at this stage, Iain made absolutely no effort to rectify our situation, and so, was as much to blame as myself and Euan.

The time for breakfast had long gone. Instead, we went looking for lunch. Stopping at the first restaurant, which had a table allowing us to keep an eye on our bikes (got to watch out for those multi-millionaire, yacht-owning bike thieves) we promptly ordered three bica, three beers, three large bottles of water, two pepperoni pizzas, and a spaghetti carbonara.

One of the great things about cycling is that on long rides, you get to eat whatever you want. (I bet Mo Farah has never stopped for a hearty meal and a couple of pints halfway through a marathon!)

The pizzas arrived promptly, but Iain was left waiting for his carbonara. They must have been waiting for a particularly special ingredient or something, because when it arrived, it certainly came loaded with one – an inordinate amount of human hair. This wasn't, like, an eyelash or a single strand – which would have been unpleasant enough. It was like someone had swept a hairdresser's floor and mixed it in with the carbonara sauce. Iain quickly lost his hunger but retained much of his anger.

Stopping for Beers in Albufeira

Every evening, during the ride, we would look at the distances we needed to cover the next day and work out approximately what time we would arrive at our destination.

This usually went somewhere along the lines of, "If we get up at six and head off before seven, stop for breakfast somewhere about nine or ten, we should get to the endpoint by around two or three in the afternoon and perhaps be able to go to the beach and have a swim before dinner."

Stupidly, we never factored in our unscheduled beer stops, some of which lasted well over an hour. Albufeira was a particularly challenging place for us to leave in 2014. There is just something that makes you want to drink your day away in Albufeira. Perhaps it was the thought of the killer climb out of the resort that made us so reticent to jump back on our bikes, and made us refill our glasses instead. What can I say? We were very easy to distract, and, unfortunately, it's not because any of us particularly loved Albufeira.

*(Okay, I'm going to throw in a **disclaimer** here quickly. Obviously, you cannot make a reasonable*

judgement on a town based on a quick bike ride through it. Yes, Albufeira is clearly a product of mass tourism, but that doesn't make it a bad place. I do have a soft spot for a number of the busier and perhaps more hedonistic resorts around Europe.

So what I'm going to ask is this: Please read what I've got to say about Albufeira, and then, instead of jumping on Facebook to call me all sorts of names (I often hang out on the Anything and Everything Algarve Facebook Group pages), please take the time to educate me on what I should see next time I'm in town.)

Many things skew my opinion about Albufeira.

First of all is the town's bullring – a building that is almost as ugly as the "sport" that is hosted within its walls. A quick look through the letters pages of the English-language press on the Algarve will reveal an ongoing debate about bullfighting in Portugal. The letter writers usually fall into two camps. First and foremost, there are the animal-loving expats (bolstered by the occasional local) who decry the activities in the bullring as the epitome of cruelty. Then, there are the avid supporters of the activity who vocally defend it and thank the expatriate community not to stick their noses into their culture. Needless to say, there is little common ground between the two groups (which probably means the letters editor of *The Portugal News* or *Algarve Resident* will never be short on work.)

Secondly – and almost as ugly as the polarizing bullring – is the multi-coloured hell of Albufeira Marina. The locals call this strip of holiday apartments and commercial properties (most of which are empty) LEGOLAND. If you suffer from migraines, it is probably best that you avoid the area altogether. I cannot imagine what the architects or local government were thinking when this monstrosity was designed and granted planning permission.

Finally – and this is perhaps the most valid reason for my feelings – I'm afraid my experience of Albufeira has been tarnished by the actions of some of my fellow countrymen, who apparently can only seem to enjoy a holiday in the resort by drinking themselves into oblivion. It's a shame to travel so far just to spend time with people whom you would cross the road to avoid back home. While I'm sure the Portuguese like taking money from these holidaymakers, I'm sure they also find them utterly tedious.

In 2014, we attracted a lot of tedious attention in Albufeira.

First, there was a man from Newcastle who kept insisting on shaking our hands and telling us what we were doing was terrific. He had no idea how far we had travelled; for all he knew, we could have just taken our bikes for a short ride to the pub. He was incredibly drunk. Far *too* drunk, considering the sun was still high in the sky. He had a real sadness in his eyes. He apparently loved the idea of going for a bike ride himself but knew that he would have to sober up first, and that wasn't likely to happen anytime soon. His wife tried for a good 20 minutes to get him to leave us alone, but to no avail.

Then there was the gang of football-obsessed fools, led by one particularly aggressive chap who loudly proclaimed they thought cycling was "gay." It's a terrible world when the worst insult you can find in your tiny mind is to question a complete stranger's sexuality. To be fair, most of the lads didn't look like they were enjoying themselves, rather like they were forced into downing pint after pint for fear of their peer group casting aspirations on their own sexuality. (It should also be said that we weren't the ones glued to a TV screen watching 22 young men chase each other around a field.)

Finally, there was a Scottish lady. Upon hearing myself, Iain, and Euan's accents, she insisted on speaking to us. She was on holiday with her extended family. They were all thoroughly pissed. Her main topic of conversation revolved around guessing how old she was. She was clearly in her late forties (which meant she didn't like it when we guessed 48). Although, I guess there is the chance she could have been prematurely aged by the vast number of cigarettes she smoked, constantly lighting a fresh one from the butt of her last. Just as we were making our excuses to leave, she jumped into the air and landed quite impressively – and without spilling a drop of her freshly-filled glass – in the full splits.

In 2018, the crowd wasn't half as entertaining.

Ready for a drink, we pulled into a bar next to a high-rise hotel that had all the charm of a multi-story carpark and quickly caught the attention of several all-day drinkers. They were harmless enough but just had this crazy idea that because we were all Brits, we would enjoy their rapier-sharp wit.

How many times can the same man ask who is winning the bike race before exploding into fits of laughter? At least five or six, apparently.

The only other topic of conversation on offer was how drunk each one of them had gotten the previous evening. These weren't kids on their first foreign adventure away from their parents, but men in their fifties and maybe even sixties. I'll be honest with you; I like a drink, and we all started each morning with a bit of a hangover on this trip, but there is nothing charming or witty about a man of a certain age bragging to his friends about throwing 100 euros over a bar before collapsing, being sick in his bath, and leaving the mess for the hotel cleaners to sort out.

I wondered if this was the only story these gentlemen would take home to their (I'm guessing estranged) families – "I went to Portugal and got pissed." It's a bit sad, really.

In all fairness, they *did* seem to have a great relationship with the young waiter who kept topping up their drinks. They apparently didn't see his smile slip from his face the moment he turned his back on the old fools.

They say the difference between a traveller and a tourist is that a traveller doesn't know where they are going, whereas a tourist doesn't know where they have been. I have evidence for this.

The little drunken party of gentlemen was joined by an equally-confused lady who told anyone who wanted to listen that she'd come out for a few drinks because her sister (whom she had come on holiday with) had apparently gone on a bus tour for the day to Valletta. I don't know where her sister had gone, but it almost certainly wasn't 3,600 km away to the island of Malta.

As we cycled away from the bar, a group of middle-aged men sat down. They were each wearing a different-coloured butcher's hat. The hats were apparently part of a "fun" theme at the centre of their holiday. However, if it was fun, someone should have told their sunburnt faces. They looked thoroughly miserable.

"Six beers, mate."

"Whoa – how pissed were we last night?"

Rinse, repeat.

Okay, while I admit that I might be being a little bit unfair to the resort of Albufeira – and maybe even some of my fellow countrymen – on my last visit just prior to writing this book, my opinion of both had been severely tarnished before I even landed in Portugal.

Ryanair flights can be a little boisterous at times, and that's understandable with lots of people excited to be going on holiday. Typically, this is all taken in good humour. However, our flight was blighted by a really loud, drunk, and offensive stag party from Oldham on their way to Albufeira. Banter is banter, but come on, people; there were families on this flight, and they didn't need to be faced with such abusive language, which included threats of sexual violence towards other passengers and individual members of the crew. Call me a snob, but I don't think Portugal needs this kind of tourism. Thankfully, in the 12+ years I've been visiting the region on a fairly regular basis, this was the first time I'd witnessed such lousy behaviour. Let's hope it doesn't become the norm.

It was time to get the hell out of Albufeira, which is a shame, because it could be quite lovely in the right company. I'll admit, I do have a rather strange affection for "bucket and spade" seaside resorts – it must be my connection to Cleethorpes.

Actually, I'm going to make a promise to give Albufeira another chance. I've been thinking about doing a solo run of the Ecovia again but in two days this time. By my "rule of thumb" measurements, that would make Albufeira the halfway point. Perhaps an overnight stay in town and a recommendation for a good restaurant and a decent bar will change my mind. In fact, I'm already playing around with book titles for the trip. Something like: *The Portugal Pie Eaters' Triumphant Return to Albufeira.*

Pop trivia fans might be interested in learning that Albufeira has a street named after the singer, Sir Cliff Richard, who, for many years, was one of the region's most famous residents. In fact, the Algarve is literally dripping with celebrity visitors and residents. The likes of British TV royalty, including Ant and Dec, Holly Willoughby, and Phillip Schofield all apparently own holiday homes on the Algarve and can regularly be seen in some of the region's swankier hangouts.

The climb out of Albufeira was our first big challenge of the trip. While Dave and Chris resorted to pushing, I was absolutely delighted to be able to ride to the top with Iain. The secret to climbing, we both smugly agreed, was not to focus on speed but just to keep a steady cadence and remember to breathe. Obviously, we were incredibly keen to pass this information on to our fellow riders at the summit. For some strange reason, Chris and Dave weren't that impressed. Perhaps they would have moved faster if they thought that Holly Willoughby was waiting for them at the top of the hill.

Stop Press: *While proofreading this book, my partner, Sarah, reminded me that we had actually visited Albufeira long before I started cycling across the Algarve. It was out-of-season, and the resort was incredibly quiet. We took a stroll into the resort and stopped for an Irish coffee at a beachfront hotel. There, we got to chatting with an incredibly drunk old lady (what is it with Portugal and old ladies?). She was easily in her late eighties or even nineties and (I thought at the time) undoubtedly glad for the company and a little conversation. I wondered if she was lonely, but she told us that she enjoyed sitting and looking out to sea, listening to the crashing waves and having a "little" drink. If people came along and they appeared friendly, she would talk to them. If not, she was happy with her own company. She was probably used to it. She told us that her son was really angry with her for going on holiday by herself – particularly, as she couldn't afford travel insurance. She couldn't see what the problem was, saying that if she dropped dead, they could throw her body into the sea. I kind of admired her badass spirit and was glad to learn she was spending her son's inheritance on enjoying herself. After all, if he was really so worried about her, couldn't he have gone on holiday with his old mother?*

Rude Lady

A change is as good as a holiday, and, as I have already alluded, change is the only constant on the Ecovia, where nothing stays the same for too long.

The boardwalk at Praia Dos Salgados Nature Reserve provided a welcome change from the dirt tracks and asphalt roads. The gentle burring sound of our bike wheels rolling across the wooden planks was incredibly relaxing.

Sharing the boardwalk with so many people on foot – including numerous children and dogs on leads – slowed us down, but we were happy to enjoy the slower pace. Contrary to popular opinion (if you read *The Daily Mail*), most cyclists really *do* enjoy sharing paths with other considerate users.

(Just for the record, my definition of "considerate" means not being mesmerised by your smartphone or letting your dog's extendable lead stretch to the other side of the path on which you are walking.)

We rode at a pace to enable those walking toward us the opportunity to stand to the side and let us pass. We employed our bells to warn those with their backs against us that we were coming through. We shared a "Hello" or an "Obrigado" and a smile with everyone we passed. Children waved; we waved back. Everyone was happy, until we got stuck behind a little family unit who were heading in the same direction, and so, had their backs to us. A mother walked hand-in-hand with her two young children, taking up the entire width of the boardwalk.

I politely rang my bell. One of the little children turned and smiled before shaking her mother's hand and highlighting that we were riding behind her. She didn't move.

Her husband directed an older child to the side of the boardwalk and smiled broadly at us, but the lady maintained her position.

After another polite ring of the bell, her other child called out to her, *"Mama, Mama, bicicleta."* Still, no movement.

Dave joined in with his bell, and I offered an "Excuse me." Nowt.

Eventually, our bells sounded like a beginners' class in campanology.

Was she blocking our path on purpose?

I am always conscious – especially when sharing paths with pedestrians – that others might have hearing or sight-relation problems. However, after carefully analysing the situation for some time, I came to the conclusion that this woman's only problem was that she was just being incredibly rude and perhaps a little overentitled.

She apparently felt that we didn't belong on the boardwalk behind her and her (much nicer) family – although it was clearly marked as a shared path.

Now, I don't want to appear rude, but, like most people I have encountered who don't like bikes, she looked like getting on a bike every now and again would probably do her a world of good.

Polite to the end, I'm sure I heard Chris shout, "Thank you" (or something similar-sounding) as we finally rode past her.

Fear of the Dark

The route into Portimão and onwards to Praia da Rocha is usually relatively sedate, but, thanks to our earlier navigational errors and an extended stop in Albufeira (where we might have considered catching a train if I hadn't told a little white lie about there not being a train station), we were running late. So late, in fact, that the sun had set, and it was dark. This wouldn't have been a problem if we weren't on an incredibly busy stretch of the N125 (why were we on the N125 again when there is a much more forgiving route?) and about to cross a suspension bridge over the Arade River, which was utterly unsuitable for bikes, especially at that time of the night.

Cars sped past us, beeping their horns and shouting at us to get off the road. We pedalled furiously. I'm quite sure we were 100% fuelled by panic.

As we crossed the river and into Portimão, I looked across at Iain.

He looked back at me angrily and shouted. "Nobody is enjoying this!"

He was wrong, because secretly, I was loving every minute of it. Besides, we were almost at our stopping point for the night. A few beers and a bite to eat, and we would all soon forget the trauma.

Iain's rage would be further tested as a car (full of, as he would call them, "neds") slowly drove past us before winding their windows down and miming a drive-by shooting. These little "gangbangers" could barely see over the steering wheel. If Iain had any energy left in his legs, he would have evidently chased them down and confronted them with raw Aberdonian rage.

Later in the evening, Iain told me his stress was compounded by the size of Portimão.

He told me he thought it would be like cycling into Muchalls (a tiny village south of Aberdeen) and not a big, sprawling city like Glasgow. For the record, Portimão is nothing like Glasgow. For instance, you're probably more likely to get stabbed in Glasgow than killed in a drive-by (joking, of course!).

The ride into Portimão and down toward Praia da Rocha in 2018 was a much more pleasant experience than our late-night, car-induced panic of 2014. The ride along the river convinced me that, should I find myself with time to kill in the area at a later date, it could well be worth exploring. It would certainly be a change from the beach. Dare I say it? It appeared to be somewhat *cultured* (although I may have reached this conclusion on the basis that nobody threatened to shoot us).

Despite this, I still have mixed feelings about Praia da Rocha. Don't get me wrong. I really like the place. I'm just not really quite sure *why* I like the place.

On the plus side, as a bustling resort, it has the feeling that something is always going on. Its beach is beautiful; if you've ever seen a stock photo of a Portuguese beach, it's probably been taken in Praia da Rocha. The beach is complemented by a lovely promenade that takes you in the direction of Alvor, which I was delighted to discover following my aborted second leg of the ride in 2012. The resort also has all the benefits of being attached to the larger city with all its conveniences.

On the more negative side, it's probably the one place on the Algarve that could give the fleshpots of Tenerife or Majorca a run for their money. It's the closest thing Portugal has got to the high-rise environment of some of the tackier Spanish resorts (don't worry, though; it's still a million miles from the concrete jungles of Benidorm or Torremolinos). The main strip and surrounding streets are home to numerous pubs and clubs, which seem to be increasingly supplemented by unsavoury-looking "gentlemen's clubs." These include the completely unalluring-sounding Lunatic Strip Club. This inevitably attracts a particular kind of tourist (many of whom might well be lunatics).

However, I think the main reason why I am so fond of Praia da Rocha is that it was the first place I ever visited in Portugal nearly 30 years ago, on one of my first foreign holidays. It's the place where I first tasted piri-piri chicken (hot, hot, hot!) and plucked and ate an orange directly from a tree (it was incredibly bitter, probably better used in marmalade). The resort introduced me to the country I now know so well and love. Undoubtedly, Praia da Rocha has changed a great deal in the years since my first visit, but, then again, *I've* also changed quite a bit. I certainly wouldn't have dreamed it would be possible to cycle the length of the Algarve 30 years ago.

The question is: While I definitely have a lot of affection for Praia da Rocha, would I ever choose to take my family there on holiday? I'm not sure. Perhaps I should keep Praia da Rocha as a guilty pleasure (and no, we never even *considered* visiting the Lunatic Strip Club).

Dave, Chris, and I stayed at the Residencial Sol right on the main strip. The hotel was rather basic, but the staff were amicable and the price of 21 euros a night was just about right for a place we would spend only six hours in. When we checked in, the receptionist warned us there was a nightclub directly across the road from the hotel that could be noisy and suggested a room at the back of the building would be more comfortable.

I asked the receptionist if the nightclub was worth visiting. She didn't respond, which was probably an excellent answer.

The porter then took us around the back of the hotel to find somewhere to secure our bikes out of sight from the revelling hordes before heading out to dinner. We locked up our bikes behind a secure wall of tea towels and bedding outside the hotel's laundry room. I normally wouldn't be too happy leaving the bikes out in the open but felt pretty confident in their security, seeing as nothing overlooked the hotel's backyard.

Iain was booked into the more luxurious Jupiter Algarve Hotel about 100 meters down the road. Iain claims he was unable to find a room at the Residencial, but I secretly think he was attracted to the hotel because of the large dance floor and "easy listening" live music that we were treated to when we joined him in the bar. The expected dress code at the Jupiter almost certainly included a smart pair of slacks, a blazer, and a necktie. We certainly stood out in our somewhat casual eveningwear. Iain smugly told us that his bike had been parked somewhere secure by a smartly-dressed valet who was incredibly polite but had a look of utter contempt in his eyes as he wheeled the dust-covered bike through the fancy hotel lobby.

Joking aside, it was nice to see Praia da Rocha catering to a more genteel class of tourists. Hopefully, the 100-metres' distance between the Residencial and the Jupiter would spare its guests from the *bang, bang, thump* of the Katedral nightclub we would later endure.

We ate on the rooftop terrace of the nearby Restaurante Cletonina, where the lads had pizza and chips (that's right; they doubled-up on carbs – which, unless you are on an extended bike ride, might just be illegal). I went for chicken in a creamy sauce and chips – which, bizarrely, came with a bib. I'm not sure whether a bib is given out to all customers, or I just looked like a messy eater.

As we were the only diners in the restaurant, the waiters – who were all really cool and certainly not pushing us out the door – looked like they might want to go home. Despite being told the kitchen was now closed, we ordered another bottle of wine.

When we finally did leave the restaurant, the staff didn't hang around and were right out the door behind us, quickly pulling down the shutters and locking up for the night. It was probably the second bottle of wine, rather than a sense of mischief, that delayed us from telling them Chris was still in the bathroom and was now trapped in the building. As the front shutter was pulled back up, Chris stood in the doorway, looking slightly confused and mildly panicked.

Although there was plenty of noise coming from the nightclub, the strip didn't seem too busy when we got back to the hotel around midnight, but clearly, the night was young.

The real noise didn't start until around 5 AM, when the club began kicking people out. We were woken by the sound of huge crowds chanting English football songs (makes you proud). Next door to the club was a large tourist information centre, which included an equally large tourist police station. It didn't sound as if the tourists who visited the strip needed too much protection (apart from themselves, maybe).

Not needing an alarm call (thanks to the clubbers), Chris had all our bikes out front by 6.30 AM. We were just getting ready to push off when a somewhat dishevelled man emerged from a bush between the club and the police station, brushed himself off, and staggered home.

Deep Heat

We exited Praia da Rocha and Portimão with a leisurely ride along the seafront before climbing out of the town, past the local airfield, and onto the N125 in the direction of Lagos for breakfast.

Lagos has to be one of my favourite stops on the western side of the Algarve. While the town is incredibly popular with tourists in the summer months, it has not gone down the slippery slope of becoming a tacky tourist resort. Yes, the beaches are lovely and there are many great places to eat, drink, and be merry, but the town has retained its "real-world" appeal.

Perhaps because of this, Lagos has become an incredibly popular destination for expats who actually want to live in Portugal, rather than just holiday there. This has inevitably pushed the price of property up.

If the east of the Algarve is too quiet for you, and the likes of Vilamoura and Albufeira are too garish and noisy, perhaps Lagos would be the perfect place for you.

As we reached the outskirts of Lagos, the guys were tempted by the golden arches of

America's finest fast food dining experience. I pretended not to hear their calls to stop and broke away at speed from the group, forcing them to follow.

Iain had been struggling with his knee, so after finding a café stop at Lagos' small but nonetheless charming marina (I think I prefer it here to Vilamoura), he enquired whether there was a pharmacy nearby.

There wasn't a pharmacy on the marina, but it did have a vending machine for essential items, including a 500 ml tube (seriously, half a litre) of anti-inflammatory muscle rub.

Chris quickly took ownership of the tube and squirrelled himself away in the bathroom. Iain, who'd followed Chris to the facilities, came back with tears of laughter rolling down his face as he described the scene.

The toilet cubicles had frosted glass doors and behind one of them, a large, naked, ginger man could be clearly seen applying lashings of lotion all over his body. (There is no truth to the rumour that Chris has started using Deep Heat recreationally since returning to the UK.)

By the way, Lazyjack's Bar and Grill in Lagos wins the best breakfast of the trip, hands down. We've got to thank the Anything and Everything

Facebook Group again for that recommendation. Who needs McDonald's?

But even an excellent recommendation for a cooked breakfast would pale when compared to the kindness of strangers, which happened within a few miles of each other over the course of our 2014 and 2018 rides.

Praia da Luz

As resorts go, there is nothing special to make Praia da Luz stand out from the hundreds of other resorts along the Algarve. It's just a quiet, unassuming place where people go to relax, enjoy their holidays, and forget their troubles.

Tragically, trouble is what many people think about when they hear the name Praia da Luz, and, sadly, it will forever be associated with the disappearance of Madeleine McCann.

We were taken into Praia da Luz by a roadside sign advertising a supermarket. I needed to refill my water bottle and really fancied an ice lolly. As we made the detour, I felt the mood of the group drop when we suddenly realised where we were.

It's funny how the name of a town can do this.

I considered how many other people felt the same way upon hearing the name "Praia da Luz". I wondered if the town's residents live under a constant cloud caused by Madeleine's disappearance in 2007.

If ever a case needed resolving more…

Then, I wondered if I would have had similar thoughts if I suddenly found myself in the Scottish town of Dunblane, or the Welsh village of Aberfan.

While whatever happened in Praia da Luz all those years ago will never (and should never) be forgotten, the town must be allowed to move on from its past, and I guess I was ashamed for thinking so morbidly when I arrived there. Upon reflection, I was pleased to see a thriving, happy little community here. Life, after all, has to go on.

Highlighting that a community isn't just a product of its history, the next time I visit Praia da Luz, I will always try to remember two very positive stories that happened in the vicinity of the resort and raise a smile.

The Kindness of Strangers #2

Euan's bike began to suffer mechanical problems. While we carried a very basic toolkit, we didn't have the equipment we needed to make a repair, and so, we left the cycle trail and freewheeled ourselves into the village of Almádena (a stone's throw across the N125 from Praia da Luz) to look for a cycle shop.

There was no cycle shop; it was a Sunday, and most of the village was closed. We approached some local *bombeiros* (firefighters) enjoying their morning coffee in the sunshine. They spoke little English, but, after some rudimentary pointing and dodgy miming, they understood our problem and set off to find a local bike mechanic. When the mechanic couldn't be found, they took us to a local bar and introduced us to its owner, a British expat called Les.

Les didn't have the tools to fix it either but had a friend called Richard, who, in his retirement, enjoyed tinkering with bikes and cars. If he couldn't fix it, the holiday would have been over for one of our group.

Not only did Richard offer to help, he told us that, if he didn't have the correct size tool (a huge Allen key) to make the repair, he would actually make one with an old bolt and a grinder.

Thirty minutes later, we were all back on the road. Richard refused to take any money and even declined the offer of a coffee for his trouble. He just wanted us to enjoy our holidays.

So, how do you repay all this kindness?

The only thing I can think of is to use this book to say "thank you" once again to the bombeiros and Richard, and suggest that if you are ever in Portugal and find yourself in Almádena, pop into Restaurante O Poco and tell Les that three Scottish cyclists who found themselves in trouble sent you there.

The Kindness of Strangers #3

There are some serious hills between Praia da Luz and Sagres. The struggle of climbing (or even pushing) can be quickly forgotten with the joy of a quick downhill ride. Unfortunately, one of my most spectacular descents was ruined by my front tube exploding, causing my tyre to deflate instantaneously.

For a seasoned cyclist like me, a flat tyre isn't a big issue. I pushed the bike to the bottom of the hill before flipping it onto its back to make the repair.

When we collected our bikes from the airport, I remember being handed a spanner, but, upon inspecting my friends' bikes (which all had quick-release wheels), I told the courier we didn't need it.

This would have been fine if (like all my friends' bikes) my bike had a quick-release wheel. It didn't, and I definitely needed that spanner.

While trying to decide what to do next, Dave produced an envelope he had been presented by the charity we were supporting, which had the words, *"Only to be opened in times of crisis"* written on it.

Undoubtedly, this was as near to a crisis as we were ever going to get on this trip.

Dave handed me the envelope, and I removed the floral-print card inside.

The card read, *"Whenever you find yourself doubting how far you can go, remember how far you've come. Remember everything you've faced, all the battles you've won, and all the fears you've overcome. The #GetYourBellyOut Community (a fundraising initiative from supporters of Crohns and Colitis UK) is with you, every step of the way. You've got this."*

The card had been signed by loads of people, which we all agreed was really nice, but joked that it was as much use to us now as a chocolate fire poker. The time for words was over; we needed a spanner.

We didn't panic and set about trying to fix the puncture without removing the wheel. The self-adhesive patches I had packed from home were next-to-useless. Next, we tried the puncture repair kits provided by the hire company, but the tubes of glue had set like rubber and were no good. I was considering tying a knot in the tube and then trying to re-inflate it or perhaps stuffing the tyre with grass (because there is always a way out of these situations) before I had the bright idea of stopping traffic – the only problem being that we were in the middle of nowhere, and there was very little traffic on the road.

We waited a couple of minutes before the first car came by. It stopped but had no toolkit. Another couple of minutes passed before another vehicle came our way and stopped. Again, the driver had no toolkit, but he *did* have an apartment 15 minutes away and promised to return with an adjustable spanner – which he duly did.

I didn't catch the gentleman's name, but he told me that he hailed from the Lincolnshire town of Sleaford, which is quite close to my hometown. Again, we had no other way of thanking him beyond words. Wouldn't it be nice if those words could be extended in the form of this book? I wonder if he will ever read it and think: *Wow, that's about me.* I challenge social media to find the #SleafordBikeHeroOnTheAlgarve and get this book into his hands.

We replaced the tube, waved our saviour off, and started climbing in the direction of Sagres, and, ultimately, Cape St Vincent.

How Much Can You Bench Press?

Another thing that will always make me raise a smile whenever I think of Praia da Luz is Dave's reaction to my ability to cycle with relative ease up the steep incline away from the supermarket we visited. As I passed him, I could hear him muttering something along the lines of, "I could bench press more than any of you." I'm not sure if any of us were meant to hear this, but we all responded with the universal "clutching my handbag" gesture followed by a perfectly chorused "ooooh!"

Dave later got his chance to showcase his bench pressing skills by helping everyone lift their bikes over a fence when we suddenly rediscovered the blue line on a sweet, sweet piece of tarmac running parallel to the N125.

Super Supermarkets

While the Algarve isn't as densely-built as the Spanish Costas, it's certainly not short of tourist-friendly places to stop along the route to top-up your water bottles or lift your morale with a quick bica and an egg custard tart. This makes it the ideal destination for entry-level (as well as more experienced) long-distance cyclists. If you are nervous about getting into trouble, or you are just not sure whether you have the strength in your legs to continue, on the Algarve, you're never very far away from civilisation and potential help.

Throughout the ride, we called in on numerous, often fairly rudimentary roadside cafes, some of them little more than a coffee machine, a large Coca-Cola fridge, a few tables on the pavement, and a large-screen television (there is always a TV tuned to a football match). In some cases, you might not be actually sure whether you have entered a commercial premises or someone's front room. The service is never hurried, and, depending on which game is being shown on the TV, sometimes appears to be somewhat grudgingly doled out. However, we always enjoyed these stops, which were often supplemented by the interest of an affectionate stray dog (which Chris inevitably made friends with) and certainly fell into the camp of an authentic Portuguese experience.

Perhaps somewhat surprisingly, another highly authentic stopping point on the route included several supermarket stops. Unlike the undoubtedly soulless experience of a trip to your local ASDA, Tesco, or (lah-de-dah!) Waitrose, the supermarkets in Portugal seem to be less sterile than their UK equivalents, and, somehow, have retained a sense of community spirit about them. What's more, the aisles are lined with fresh food, while real butchers and fishmongers ply their trade, offering their customers a personal and informed service. The various deli and hot food counters provide a fantastic array of food. On my last visit, this included perfectly-grilled spatchcock chicken (not dripping with grease like the roasted birds on offer in UK supermarkets). I've even seen a whole, ready-cooked suckling pig. If you're trying to cut costs and eat out of supermarkets, it doesn't mean you'll be restricted to bread and cheese. (Incidentally, the bread in Portugal is to die for. Try spreading some sardine pate on a thick slice of freshly-baked bread and you'll never look at a jar of Shipman's fish paste again. It's also worth noting that Portuguese tomatoes literally explode with taste and are nothing like the tasteless, watery variety we're used to in the UK.)

The supermarkets inevitably have a café with proper barista coffee (no dodgy automated machines here) and a great selection of cakes and pastries. We spent several stops refuelling at a supermarket café, and taking our drinks and snacks out to the tables that were often set up in the car park. Back home, I would never consider hanging out outside my local Aldi. In Portugal, it seems perfectly natural.

Where Did Those Hills Come From?

In 2012 and 2014, without the aid of the BikeGPX app, we pretty much stuck to the N125 between Lagos and Sagres. The "death road" proved to be reasonably efficient at flattening out any bumps on the hilliest section of the ride.

However, what the N125 took away from the ride in terms of climbs, it certainly added to in terms of monotony. The N125 is basically a joyless experience. In 2018, we had the technology to take us on a more interesting route, which I was glad of.

As we climbed away from the coast, some of the views were absolutely staggering, but this reward cost us dearly in terms of climbs. Just as you thought the road couldn't go any higher another, hill came into view. While Iain was undoubtedly the "King of the Mountains" on this ride, he soon joined Dave in lobbying for a return to the more monotonous but less hilly N125 – which I rallied against for as long as I could.

As we wound our way through the Portuguese countryside, moving away from the coast for prolonged periods of time, it wasn't always obvious that we were heading in the right direction.

I personally put all my faith into the GPS on my smartphone, but my fellow riders began to doubt my sense of direction. At one stage, Chris pulled a compass out of his panniers. I'm not sure why he packed it, but the crew gathered around him, seeking his navigational wisdom.

He asked us which direction we thought north was. We all pointed in different directions.

In all the confusion, I was reminded of a TV documentary about an entire squadron of aircraft lost in the Bermuda Triangle after losing faith in their instruments and foolishly trusting their instincts.

It took some persuasion to remind the guys that GPS is a pretty reliable tool, but, eventually, faith in our Bike GPX maps was restored.

The Germans, the Australians, and the Albufeira Cycling Club

Cyclists are inevitably drawn to other cyclists. What can I say? We are nice people. During our various trips across the Algarve, several groups of cyclists stuck out in my mind.

First were the Germans, whom we met in 2014. We just kept bumping into them over the three days we were on the road. They were following the same schedule as us and always had a cheery wave, a bright *"Hallo"* and the occasional, cheeky *"Das ist gut."* We would often joke with them that they were responsible for getting us lost, or accuse them of following us.

The Germans were a father-and-son team. The father must have been in his eighties and was evidently much fitter than any of us. No eBike required there. I've got to admit that I found him incredibly inspiring and hope that I'm still capable of riding the Algarve when I am his age. I know it is something I would have loved to share with my father before he passed away. I also hope that, one day, my daughters will want to indulge me by joining me on a bike ride in my dotage.

Then, in 2018, in very similar circumstances, we met a husband-and-wife team from Australia, who, like the Germans, just kept appearing along the route. Somewhat comically, this always seemed to be while we were resting at the top of a hill. The husband would join us for a chat, take a sip of water, and maybe eat an energy bar while waiting for his wife to reach the summit some minutes later. As soon as she did, he would set right off, not giving his wife even the briefest of moments to recover. She didn't seem so chatty. I guess chivalry has some way to go down under, but when all was said and done, you had to admire her stamina.

Then, there was the Albufeira Cycling Club. This group of "elite" cyclists (certainly compared to us) in their matching club gear and high-spec machines could have sneered at our lack of prowess and left us eating dust on our rental bikes, but happily rode alongside us for ten minutes or so, helpfully pointing us in the right direction and taking an interest in our ride.

As I've already mentioned, I believe there is far too much snobbery in cycling. Back home, I recall the first time I replaced my hybrid bike with a road bike and was amazed at the number of MAMILs who had previously ignored me on my regular weekend jaunts who suddenly started to say "Hi." I guess the drop handlebars signified some sort of club membership. If only they know I'd bought the bike from a catalogue retailer for less than £300. I could imagine the sneers. These would be amplified if they knew I was dressed exclusively in Aldi and Sports Direct clothing. I say, forget the bike, forget the gear, forget the speed you are travelling, and just enjoy that there is more that unites us than divides us. In my eyes, the Albufeira Cycling Club were perfect ambassadors for my vision of a utopian cycling world.

This reminded me of the famous H.G. Wells quote: *"Cycle tracks will abound in Utopia."* The rural backroads and dirt paths of the Algarve might be a long way from the science fiction writer's idea of the future, but I'll happily endorse the Ecovia as my idea of Utopia.

It also made me think that I really, REALLY should give Albufeira another go.

Praia da Salema

Having read a lot of cycle-related travelogues, I'm conscious of a fact that I see all too often. The start of the book is always incredibly detailed and focuses in great depth on all aspects of the ride. However, as the book progresses, details often start to get a little hazy as the writer hurries towards the end.

One of the many things that inspired me to write this book was reading the thoroughly enjoyable book, *Along the Med on A Bike Called Reggie* by Andrew P. Sykes, which documents the author's 6,000 km ride from the southern tip of Greece to the Atlantic coast of Portugal.

I read the book by the pool on a family holiday in Portugal and could feel my legs turning with the author's as he pushed his way along the coast of the continent. I was naturally excited about Mr. Sykes' take on the Portuguese section of the ride.

However, I couldn't help feeling that the author glossed over what I obviously considered to be an incredibly important part of the ride. Portugal barely got a mention.

I think I understand why he did this. By the time you get to the last stretch of a long ride (and I'm by no way comparing my little jaunts across Portugal to his incredible journey), you just start focusing on completing the ride. Nothing else matters, and, inevitably, research and the documentation process goes out the window.

In many ways, completing a trip can be a bit of a downer. There is suddenly less to look forward to, and you just want to get on with it.

Yes, we were still happy to be on the road and enjoying each other's company (apart from in 2012, when I was probably bonking, and, therefore, contemplating lying down beside the road and quietly dying), but we were now almost certainly on what I would call a mission, rather than a jolly cycle ride.

By the time we reached the beautiful village of Salema, we were all beginning to feel a little too jaded to really enjoy it. We decided to cheer ourselves up by stopping at a mini-market and spoiling ourselves with another ice lolly and a can of Sumol (a Portuguese soft drink with a little more fruit and a lot less fizz than a can of Fanta). The only problem was that we couldn't seem to get our mojo back again. We loitered outside the shop with no other real purpose but to delay the inevitable – getting back on our bikes. Chris even wrote a postcard home (who still does that?).

Praia da Salema looked like it might be a nice place to stop and explore further (at least, further than the mini-market), had time been on our side. It was certainly very pretty, retaining much of the charm lost in other resorts along the coast by overstuffing them full of holiday homes and apartment buildings.

Sadly, our only real memory of Praia da Salema was the hellish climb out of the village. At one stage of the climb, the hill was so steep that we all had to dismount and push, and the angle of the climb seemed to stretch our calve muscles to their limits.

(It's probably at this stage of the book that I should apologise to Dave and admit that there are some hills in Portugal.)

Upon connecting with the N125 again, we decided to put the hills behind us and get some respite from the ups and downs of the minor roads on the official route, swapping steep climbs for unvarying monotony.

Surf's Up

We left the N125, re-joining the Ecovia (courtesy of Dave's bench-pressing skills as he lifted our bikes over a wire fence) and perhaps the most rewarding stretch of dedicated cycle path, taking us down into the town of Sagres. These perfect cycling conditions – somewhat sheltered from the wind and largely downhill – let us pick up speed and put the memories of those recent hills and the boring, old road behind us.

Sagres appears to be a really cool town (so cool, it has a beer named after it). Given a chance, I would love to spend some more time there. The Atlantic coast of Portugal has a reputation for being a remarkable surfing destination, boasting some of the biggest waves in the world. While many of the resorts along the Algarve coast have been designed with golfers in mind (which has gone a long way to making the Algarve a year-round holiday destination, also ideally suited to cycling), in my opinion, Sagres definitely has the cooler surf crowd in mind.

I'm not a surfer myself, but I can certainly appreciate the sport. Unlike golf, the surfer's environment is not one that has been tamed and manicured. In fact, it's probably a case of "the wilder, the better". It's a sport which exemplifies complete freedom – which, in many ways, makes me think that cyclists and surfers are cut from the same cloth.

However, there is one problem with Sagres: It doesn't have a train station. When everyone drives the obligatory surfer's VW camper van, why would you need a train station? This means that if you are running on the same three-day schedule as we were, there is no time to stop and explore. This is because you've got to give yourself enough time to get to the end point at Cape St. Vincent before turning back and cycling the 34 km back to Lagos if you are going to catch your train back to Faro. This is a fact I forgot to tell Chris and Dave about before getting them to commit to the ride. They might have thought they'd finished the ride at Cape St. Vincent – think again.

Just days before our arrival in Portugal, Chris actually asked me via the WhatsApp group if "the bus" would meet us at the end point. A bloody bus! Where did he think that was coming from? Did he think he was on holiday?

Into The Wind

With time not on our side, we pushed on relentlessly towards what perhaps we should call the ceremonial end of the ride.

The last 5 km towards the Cape is tough. Not because it's particularly hilly (because it's not). It's got more to do with the wind blowing in off the Atlantic. These conditions make the west coast of Portugal ideal for big wave surfing but not so great for cycling.

Riding into a constant headwind is like riding through thick treacle. It saps your energy and just makes you want to give up. It's also incredibly difficult to work out distances as the flat, cliff-top terrain doesn't really give anything away.

As you cycle from Sagres towards the Cape, the lighthouse which marks the most southwestern point of Europe is in clear view, but it doesn't appear to get any closer until the very last moment.

As you draw ever closer to the end, you start competing for space on the road with camper vans (these are like cockroaches on the Algarve) and tourist buses, packed with tourists desperate to look out across the ocean at a new, unseen world. (The next landmass from here is America.)

The end of the route is marked by nothing more than a large, metal sign and a rusty-looking bike sculpture. While the cliffs are a fantastic sight (especially with locals sat fishing with their feet dangling over the 75-metre drop), the actual endpoint of the ride is a bit of an anti-climax (isn't life always that way?). There's very little here but a smattering of market stalls selling the usual tourist tac, and – the highlight of our day – a food truck, promising the last hot dog in Europe. Okay, admittedly, you can visit the lighthouse, but let's be honest; isn't the real purpose of a lighthouse to keep people as far away from it (and the rocks it highlights) as possible?

Of course, the real reason behind the anticlimactic feeling was that the ride was almost done. Yes, we'd gone there to cycle the length of the Algarve (which we did), but the real pleasure was in the shared experience and the bonds of friendship that a trip like this will seal for life. In less than 24 hours, this would all be behind us, and we'd be flying back to our everyday lives – the commute to work, paying the mortgage, doing the big shop, cutting the grass, and a whole 12 months (or maybe more) before we'd all hopefully be doing this again. We were all tired, we were all sore (apart from Chris, who could no longer feel his entire body after covering it in anti-inflammatory muscle rub), but we would all have added an extra day to the journey, given half a chance. Finishing a ride is a bit like finishing a book that you don't want to end; it can be a real downer.

In 2012, with nobody to celebrate my partial victory with (well, I *did* cover two-thirds of the route), I tried to make conversation with some bike packers who'd arrived a couple of minutes behind me. I asked them how far they had travelled. Their kit looked like it had cost more than my mortgage. They looked at my hire bike and cheap Raleigh panniers and blanked me. What did I say about snobbery in cycling?

2014 and 2018 were marked by a series of high-fives, some manly hugs, and the obligatory selfie to post on Facebook (because if it's not published on social media, it clearly didn't happen).

In 2018, we had an additional reason to celebrate. We'd managed to raise £1,300 for our charity, Crohns and Colitis UK. Dave, as the catalyst for the ride, had chosen this charity after a close friend was hospitalised and very nearly died of the disease a number of years earlier. If you are interested in how we raised this money,

I've included a brief guide at the back of this book.

Several weeks after the ride, I saw Dave's friend tag him in a post on Facebook, saying we had inspired her to take on a 150-mile ride – which, with the aid of a ton of pain medication, she'd completed in three weeks. She had since started lobbying Dave (who wasn't a cyclist, if you recall) to buy a bike and start going on some rides with her. I'm probably more proud that we inspired someone to do something so positive for themselves and get on a bike than I am of the ride.

There was only one thing left to complete the ride – a celebratory hot dog.

Somewhat comically, you get a certificate highlighting that you have eaten at the last hotdog stand in Europe when you stop here. However, I couldn't help feeling a little cheated. I wonder if they would consider offering something extra (perhaps a little plastic medal) for those who had cycled there, rather than taken a tourist bus. The achievements just don't seem comparable.

In 2018, the Portugal Pie Eaters swapped their pies for hotdogs and proudly received three certificates each before jumping back on our bikes. Although we'd reached our final destination, we still had quite some ways to go before we got home.

The Long Ride Back

What was I saying about the headwind when cycling towards the Cape? It appears to come from such a strange direction that, even when travelling in the opposite direction, it never really gets behind you.

In 2014, we were struggling, and time wasn't on our side. We had just a couple of hours to get back to Lagos to catch the last train back to Faro. With early-morning flights booked, missing the train wasn't an option. We had barely reached Sagres, when Iain and Euan disappeared from view.

30 minutes passed before I managed to get Euan on the phone. Iain had suffered a flat tyre and was struggling to fix it – although, I'm not sure how much of an effort they really made. They had taken the executive decision that they were both happy to have completed the ride and would now be taking a taxi back to the train station in Lagos.

They asked me if I wanted to come back and share it with them, but after my incomplete ride two years earlier, I desperately wanted to end the ride on my own terms. For me, the Cape was not the final destination. I pushed on and forced myself to ride hard into the wind.

It was another 30 minutes before Iain and Euan passed me in their taxi. The car drove alongside me while they confirmed that I was okay to continue by myself and then sped off in the direction of Lagos. For a moment, I felt like Bradley Wiggins, cycling alongside his support vehicle in the Tour de France. The pressure was on, but I was loving every minute of it. Okay, I'd never win any time trial, but for once in my life, I felt fast.

As I turned my bike back into Lagos for the second time that day, the taxi whizzed past me again on his way back home to Sagres, the driver beeping his horn and flashing his lights in encouragement while wearing a massive smile on his face and waving like a maniac. I've said it before; people are nice. I held my first in the air to salute the driver and pushed on with renewed vigour.

This was, of course, helped by it being a lot easier to cycle down into Lagos than up and out of the city. Despite this, I knew I would be cutting it fine to catch my train, and, therefore, the promise of a refreshing drink back at the marina was not going to happen.

Pulling into the train station with minutes to spare, I found Iain and Euan, waiting for me with a bag full of cold beers for the journey back to Faro, and all was good with the world.

Coming Down

The only downside to cycling the Ecovia is, even on the off-chance that the weather isn't too good (surely, a once-in-a-lifetime occurrence on the sunny Algarve), the short ride is just *too* damn short.

The Portugal Pie Eaters WhatsApp group has almost certainly been more active since returning to the UK than it ever was before the trip. I guess this highlights two things: First and foremost, our lack of planning, which was quite spectacular; and secondly, how much we all wished we were back on the Algarve.

A funny thing about all our rides across the Algarve was that we never really talked much about cycling. Our bikes were just a means to an end, or merely the machines that facilitated our experience.

In 2018, amongst other things, we talked a lot about work. We all worked, one way or another, with computers, and I think the experience of being out on the route and away from technology had focused our minds on how good life was away from the glare of a laptop screen.

Inevitably, our minds focused on how we could share our experience of the ride with likeminded individuals. Was there an opportunity to start a business offering digital detox packages to burnt-out executives hoping to escape the corporate hamster wheel?

It wouldn't be too hard to set up. We'd just need to partner with a bike hire company, book a few hotels, and then build a website before marketing and selling the hell out of it. Then again, that sounded a bit too much like the work we were trying to escape from (albeit just for a long weekend).

I'm not sure if helping people get lost on a bike is such a good business idea. The cost of public liability insurance alone would be crippling enough, and I'm sure that participation in one of our "holidays" would almost certainly invalidate any standard travel insurance policy.

We needed a new business idea.

Of course, many of our "best" ideas were lubricated by our occasional libations.

After a few drinks in Faro, Chris shared his dream of opening a pizza restaurant. His concept was based on his experience of working in a pizza shop as a teenager. A regular customer would often call into the shop and demand his pizza to be cut into eight slices. On one occasion, Chris cut the pizza into just six slices, and, as a result, had the pie thrown back in his face. The experience – much like the cheese and ham topping in his hair – stuck with him for a long time, until, many years later, he formulated a business plan that would not look out of place on an episode of "Dragons' Den".

The restaurant (which our enthusiasm for the idea quickly turned into an international chain) would be called Pieces of Eight, and it would have a pirate theme, with all the staff dressed as salty sea dogs or buxom wenches (not sure if this would get past the PC brigade).

We were all sold on the idea. Had we not been on a self-imposed digital detox and bothered to check Google, we'd have seen that Chris' idea was far from original – with both Pieces of Eight and our alternative name, Pizzas of Eight, both taken.

I'm pretty sure that Chris' idea actually predated both of the businesses that had adopted it. The moral of the story is: Never sit on an idea, because it won't wait for you.

After a few more drinks (a word of warning: an Espresso Martini is a really dangerous drink to end the night on), the conversation disintegrated into the usual topics of religion, politics, and falling in love with strippers (everyone apparently has a "friend" this has happened to).

However, not everyone in our company seemed to be having such a good time.

As we talked, laughed, and cried our way through the night, a middle-aged couple sat across from us and didn't say a word to each other all night. Had they really exhausted a lifetime of chat? My advice to them is, if they really want to rekindle the art of conversation and perhaps even save their relationship, they should go on a bike ride together.

There was, of course, one more topic of conversation: Next year.

So, where to next for the Portugal Pie Eaters?

There's talk of Majorca and Tenerife (both famous for their hills). Then, there is Belgium and Holland, which should both be a bit flatter (that will please Dave) – although, I'm told both can be incredibly windy. Chris has even suggested a trip down through the Western Isles of Scotland and wild camping on beaches along the route, which might need some careful planning due to the shorter summer season.

I've also got to remember my promise to the good people of Albufeira. To be honest, there is very little that will keep me away from Portugal and the Algarve for too long.

Regardless of the destination, I'm sure the memories will write themselves.

An Education

Every minute of every day spent on a bike is an education.

When I was 30, I was diagnosed with high blood pressure. I'm guessing a mix of hereditary and lifestyle factors sent it soaring to dangerous heights. Being a bit of a hypochondriac at the best of times, I didn't take the news very well.

For an incredibly long time following the diagnosis, I convinced myself that I wasn't going to be around for too much longer and was about to be cut down in my prime by a heart attack or stroke.

Depression led to weight gain, and that led to more depression. You get the picture – all this wasn't helping my blood pressure, or my general health.

Buying a bike turned my life around and let me take back control of the situation.

Having not ridden a bike for more than 15 years, at first, I struggled to pedal five miles along the beach close to where I live. I was gradually able to increase my stamina and distances up to the stage where I now think nothing of doing a

50+ mile ride at the weekend, and I have also become a proud member of the 100-mile club (albeit a very slow 100 miles).

The more I cycled, the healthier and happier I became. It also helped me create space in my mind to be more creative and productive at work (I should invoice them for the hours I spend on my bike). As someone who earns a living as a writer, this is invaluable.

Cycling in Portugal helped me develop my passion for cycling that little bit further. It enabled me to add a little adventure to my life. Seriously, who has real adventures these days?

It also showed me that I was capable of doing anything I set my mind to. Sure, I didn't cycle around the world, or even across Europe, but if I had the time and the inclination (which I think I might do), then with a little preparation and a little planning (might need some help there), I'm sure I could do it.

It also helped me push fear to the back of my mind. Now, I think: *What's the worst that can happen?*

In reality, the worst that can happen is just as likely to happen closer to home. In my mind, that is going under a bus, and there is never really a good place for that to happen. If it's going to happen (and I hope it doesn't), Portugal is as good or as bad a place as anywhere else. Everything else is manageable if you throw enough thought (and, occasionally, money) at it.

Cycling in Portugal has also brought me closer to my friends, whom I do not get to see as often as I would like.

My goals and achievements have become *their* goals and achievements, and no matter what life throws at us, we will always have Portugal.

Sure, I still have high blood pressure (which is controlled by drugs), but I don't let it control me, because as long as I have a bike, I can do whatever I want, knowing that it will only make me stronger.

Where will your next bike ride take you?

Let me know by getting in touch on Twitter: @john_w_hayes

Online Fundraising: Five Tips for Success

Although fundraising was not my primary reason for wanting to cycle across Portugal again, it was certainly the catalyst for the ride in 2018.

Before setting off on the ride, we'd set a fundraising goal of £1,000 and threw up a webpage on JustGiving.com.

Dave used the charitable aspect of the ride as his key motivation. He was so determined not to let anyone down that he promised to match every penny donated if he failed to complete the ride. As we eventually topped £1,300, this was no small boast.

Fundraising is difficult for a number of reasons. From money being tight to a bout of compassion fatigue or a general lack of interest (fundraising is a competitive business, and sometimes, it seems like everyone is asking for money), there are a million reasons someone will find it easy to say no to your campaign.

Online fundraising should never be seen as the digital equivalent of shaking a collection tin at anyone who walks by – this approach will always be limited in its success. Online fundraisers have access to the same sophisticated content marketing arsenal as big businesses, so there is no reason why their efforts cannot be more sophisticated.

So, how can you make your campaign stand out from the crowd and keep the money coming in? I've compiled five tips I learned from the experience to ensure your campaign delivers more than just goodwill.

Five Tips for Success

1. **Build A Team:** Teamwork really does make the dream work. Even the smallest of teams, pushing out to their various networks, will help you reach a more sizeable and potentially lucrative audience. Individual successes will inspire others to make a more concentrated effort and help lift spirits on days when others aren't doing so well. Adding Chris and Iain to our team in 2018 almost certainly doubled our charity haul.

2. **Tell A Story:** Successful fundraising starts with a good story. Tell people what inspired you to work toward your current goal and how previous efforts have really

helped make a difference. And, whenever possible, focus on the positive. Even in the direst of situations, you can nearly always find a positive story of hope, achievement, or humanity. Don't just focus on social media to share your story. Build a blog (JustGiving.com has the functionality to do this), and you'll find it easier to acquire new email subscribers and build real relationships with your supporters.

3. **Focus on People:** Just like in business, people "buy" from people they like, aspire to be like, and identify with, so try to focus on people, and their hopes and aspirations for the future. These are much easier to identify with than a cash target.

4. **Document Everything:** If you are building up to a big fundraising event (for example, running a half-marathon or doing a long-distance cycle ride), document everything you do in preparation. Go crazy on social media with photographs, video, GIFs, and social stories, and encourage your supporters to share in your progress. Every piece of "marketing collateral" should always have a link to learn more or donate, but this should almost appear secondary to the story of your fundraising

efforts. Like all good content marketing, the story will "sell" the cause for you, and you'll hardly need to ask for help.

5. **Keep Your Supporters in the Loop:** A timely email to your list of supporters, updating them of your efforts, sharing campaign progress, or merely saying "thank you" will go a long way to building a robust network of supporters you can rely on in future campaigns. Remember, these aren't just people you can go to when you need money. They have bought a stake in your campaign and will want to know how well their money is being spent.

For more information about Crohn's and Colitis UK, please visit:
https://www.crohnsandcolitis.org.uk/

Acknowledgments

This book wouldn't have been possible without the following people:

A big "thank you" to my fellow Portugal Pie Eaters: Iain, Euan, Chris, and Dave. We're not an exclusive club, and new members are always welcome, so I'm looking forward to introducing new members on subsequent rides. This includes my passport-less brother, Allan.

I'd also like to extend a huge "thank you" to everyone who supported our charity ride in 2018. The generosity of friends and complete strangers serves to remind us that the world is a much nicer place than it is often made out to be. This was, of course, amplified by the individuals who came to our aid on all three rides and showed acts of human kindness that the rides would almost certainly have failed without.

A big "hello" and "thank you" to everyone on the Anything and Everything Algarve Facebook Group, who helped with research, route changes, early morning café recommendations, offers of support, and charitable donations. Social media has been getting a lot of negative press recently.

These guys showed me how positive an online community can be.

I would also like to extend my eternal gratitude to my partner, Sarah, and our two children, Rose and Dotty, who tolerate and actively encourage my cycling habit. I'd also like to thank Sarah's mum and dad, Barry and Mary, for the frequent use of their gorgeous apartment in Cabanas de Tavira, a place we have come to think of our Portuguese home-away-from-home.

Finally, I would like to thank Christina Dias and Fernando Canteiro at MegaSport Travel, our kind sponsors of this book. We rented bikes from MegaSport for all three rides featured in this book, and the company also graciously provided me with a bike to help sew up a few loose ends with my research (basically, an excuse to do a little more cycling along the Algarve).

About MegaSport Travel

MegaSport is a tour operator for walking and cycling tours in Portugal and Europe.

Supporters of environmental sustainability practices, we specialise in organising nature programs, both guided and self-guided, for individuals or groups, family holidays, and tailor-made experiences, like cycling tours in Portugal and Europe. With great knowledge of the region, we organize all the details for our programs: Bicycles, accommodation, transfers, daily luggage transfers, road books, GPS, and travel packs with privileged information to make your Portugal cycling holidays a success.

Our international and Portugal cycling and walking programs are designed to provide customers with memorable and joyful moments of relaxation, adventure, or sports during their holidays. In addition, we offer daily bicycle rental services and tours with delivery and collection, and unique Portugal cycling holidays that will create everlasting memories.

Web: www.megasportravel.com/
Email: info@megasportravel.com
Facebook: facebook.com/megasport.portugal
Tel: +351 289 393 044

Pre-ride briefing at Manchester Airport

All smiles at Faro Airport

The starting point (still smiling!) – Vila Real de Santo António

The first casualty – Fuseta

Day 2 - Escaping Faro

Messy eater – Praia da Rocha

Early doors – Praia da Rocha

Carefully-controlled diet – Lagos

Okay, there are some hills in Portugal

This is what success looks like – Cape St. Vincent

Printed in Poland
by Amazon Fulfillment
Poland Sp. z o.o., Wrocław